Bureaucrats and Brainpower: Government Regulation of Universities

BUREAUCRATS AND BRAINPOWER: GOVERNMENT REGULATION OF UNIVERSITIES

Paul Seabury, *Editor*

Nathan Glazer

Richard W. Lyman

Robert L. Sproull

Miro M. Todorovich

Caspar W. Weinberger

Introduction by Robert S. Hatfield

Institute for Contemporary Studies
San Francisco, California

Copies of this book may be purchased from the institute for $6.95. All inquiries, book orders, and catalog requests should be addressed to the Institute for Contemporary Studies, Suite 811, 260 California Street, San Francisco, California 94111—(415) 398-3010.

Library of Congress Catalog Number 79-51328
ISBN 0-917616-35-9

CONTENTS

CONTRIBUTORS

NATHAN GLAZER
Professor of Education and Sociology, Harvard University

ROBERT S. HATFIELD
Chairman and Chief Executive Officer, The Continental Group, Inc.

RICHARD W. LYMAN
President, Stanford University

PAUL SEABURY
Visiting Scholar, Hoover Institution, Professor of Political Science, UC–Berkeley

ROBERT L. SPROULL
President and Chief Executive Officer, University of Rochester

MIRO M. TODOROVICH
Assistant and Associate Professor of Physics, Bronx Community College, CUNY

CASPAR W. WEINBERGER
Vice President, Director, and General Counsel, The Bechtel Group of Companies

PREFACE

When the institute was developing its first book on regulation—*Regulating Business: The Search for an Optimum*—we considered including a chapter on the regulation of higher education in order to compare and to contrast regulation of education and of business, and to emphasize the commonality of concern. After consulting with our cosponsor on the project, the Graduate School of Management at Northwestern University, we abandoned the idea—partly for want of space, and partly because the book's format did not lend itself to that purpose.

To reflect our continuing interest in the growth of regulation, the present book is a natural sequel. It begins by exploring the narrow problems of higher education—policies on affirmative action, increasing control of research on human subjects, regulation of the natural sciences, health, and safety—and their effects on teaching, scholarship, and the integrity of universities. It then discusses the overall concern with the general increase of regulation in U.S. society, and the common purpose of academics and businessmen in dealing with it. As in our earlier book on business, attention focuses not on criticizing regulation per se, since regulation has produced palpable benefits. Rather is the book concerned with exploring the costs and benefits of particular regulations, always inquiring when and in what ways the costs of particular regulations exceed the benefits.

For this purpose, we asked Paul Seabury, who has written widely on these subjects, to bring together a group of contributors who are—or have been—involved in different aspects of the regulatory process. As a result, we have two university presidents, three public policy scholars, and a former secretary of HEW who administered many aspects of the regulation. We also have a businessman concerned with the common problems of academe and the business world.

The book's principal conclusions are clear: the recent growth of government interference in colleges and universities is threatening the autonomy and integrity of a precious national resource; without fundamental rethinking of the regulatory trends, the traditional character of higher education in this country will be changed. Parallel to this (and emphasized especially in Robert Hatfield's introductory chapter) is a growing awareness by both academics and businessmen that—although their situations are not identical—they suffer a common problem in the growth of bureaucratic regulation of all aspects of our society. In a sense, this commonality of interest may be the most important insight to be drawn from this book. That interest brings together two communities which often have been at odds in the past, but which now may have a unique opportunity for mutual understanding and cooperation.

The stake that academics have in opposing excessive regulation of universities is obvious. Less obvious, but no less important, is the stake that *businessmen* have in taking a strong public position. As Hatfield writes:

> Businessmen have a rare opportunity to become central spokesmen in a policy debate of great importance to the entire country. The reason is that reducing regulatory pressures on colleges and universities will reduce government's tendency to regulate. When businessmen speak for higher education, therefore, they will also, indirectly, be speaking for business.

This issue is important, as education is important. At a broader level, it is important as part of a general problem of growing regulation and bureaucracy in American society.

H. Monroe Browne
President,
Institute for Contemporary Studies

San Francisco, California
June 1979

INTRODUCTION

Regulating the University: A Businessman's Perspective

Regulatory expansion—its benefits and its threats. The costs in time, money, autonomy. Suggested alternatives: political activism, cooperation with government agencies, special interest groups. The opportunity for businessmen.

Government regulation of the private sector of American society has grown at an alarming rate in the past decade and a half. The problem began with the older economic regulations of private business, and in the past ten years has expanded to include social regulation of health, safety, and the environment.

Until recently, complaints about the growth of regulation—its costs and its threats to freedom—came almost exclusively from business, the first and most heavily regulated segment of society. No longer. Excessive government regulation is now an issue for everyone—and by no means a simple one.

For these reasons, I am especially pleased and proud to contribute these few observations to *Bureaucrats and Brainpower: Government Regulation of Universities*.

In later years the regulatory problem has become particularly acute in higher education. The recent history of federal regulation of higher education shows that colleges and universities are well on their way to being caught in a trap from which there may be no escape. Not long ago they were exempt from almost all federally mandated social programs, including even social security and unemployment insurance. In the mid-1960s things began to change, with the adoption of civil rights legislation banning discrimination on the basis of race, color, religion, or national origin. And soon came requirements for developing and achieving goals for hiring minorities. Gender was then added to the list, followed by age and, more recently, by physical and mental handicaps. In 1969 the National Labor Relations Board extended coverage of federal collective bargaining laws to college and university faculties, clearing the way for the faculty unionization movement. These laws and regulations were aimed not at campuses specifically, but at broad social problems; colleges and universities were either caught in the net or included by subsequent actions.

The 1974 Buckley Amendment to the Family Rights and Privacy Act began a new stage of regulation aimed *directly* at higher education. This was followed by a new version of the Health Professions Educational Assistance Amendments, which attempted to alter admissions patterns in medical schools. The Rehabilitation Act required institutions to accommodate the handicapped, and many more such laws and regulations found their way onto the books. The combined effect of these regulations on American higher education is more important than the effect of any one of them. No aspect of academic life remains unaffected. Regulations now cover hiring, promotion, and firing of personnel (including professors); wage and salary administration; pensions and personnel benefits; plant construction and management; record keeping; research; admissions; financial aid; athletics; fund raising; and even, to a degree, curricula and programs. Education, says Stanford University's vice president for public affairs Robert Rosenzweig, has finally lost its "immunity to the burdens" of an increasingly regulated society.

Some of this regulation has brought undeniable benefits. Much of the progress made in providing admission to disadvantaged students and assuring equal enrollment and employment rights to minorities and women resulted from federal funding and federal regulation. Federal programs such as the Fund for the Improvement of Postsecondary Education have served as catalysts for innovative instructional methods that might not otherwise have found their way onto the college campus. These are examples of regulation working at its best, and they should be supported by all sectors of society.

Despite the successes, however, much of the recent growth of regulation is threatening the traditional role and function of higher education. At this point, no college or university administrator needs to be reminded of the effects of bureaucratic control. Dennis F. Kinlaw, president of Asbury College in Wilmore, Kentucky, has said,

> The careful respect by government for the independence of the educational world is gone. Non-involvement has changed to intrusion, respect to financial and regulatory control. The extent is frightening.

The problem is not limited to large universities, which receive the lion's share of federal dollars. Every institution of higher learning is affected—large and small, private and public, liberal arts and technical, community college and professional school.

To me, the extent of government regulation *is* frightening. Today at least thirty-four congressional committees and seventy-four subcommittees are concerned with some hundred and fifty laws affecting higher education, and in the past dozen years the number of pages of federal law regarding higher education has grown from 90 to 360. From 1965 to 1977 the number of pages in the *Federal Register* devoted to regulations of higher education grew from 92 to more than 1,000—more than a tenfold increase.

As a result, many members of the university community have come to share business and industry's view of the excesses of government. They have discovered that federal regulatory compliance demands more than its share of the scarce dollars and valuable time of administrators and faculty, gives rise to layers of bureaucracy both in Washington and on the campus, intrudes upon internal decision-making and erodes autonomy, and leads to complicating and costly side effects such as increased litigation. They have learned that all too often bureaucrats require the gathering of useless data, cause processing delays, and play cat-and-mouse games over enforcement. What was once a theoretical problem for most colleges and universities is now a major obstacle to maintaining—even more, to improving—the quality of instruction and research.

And not only are colleges and universities faced with the soaring cost of regulatory compliance, they are now seeing their long-accepted academic freedom called into question. Traditionally, they have served as custodians of free speech and free thought. But legislation and regulation now threaten institutional freedom and autonomy. Says Estelle Fishbein, general counsel at the Johns Hopkins University,

> Manufacturers and retail establishments may be regulated and constricted, yet the business of production and buying and selling can still go on. But if regulation of the university inhibits intellectual

inquiry, if it suppresses the free exercise of intellectual judgment and the responsible exercise of discretion, then the business of the university is concluded.

Other sectors of society, including business, look to academia for broad-ranged research; colleges and universities must be vigilant that government never infringe on it.

The outlook for the future isn't very bright. New regulations continue to be written and existing ones expanded, while compliance costs rapidly increase. Frustrated and annoyed by these restraints, academia is beginning to speak out. Their voices join the chorus of other men and women, many from business, protesting increasing bureaucracy. Thus it is not uncommon to hear words like these, delivered by a spokesman for the Ivy League institutions and Stanford before the Senate Subcommittee on Education:

> We object to the increasing propensity of the federal government to intrude randomly into the day to day operation of our colleges and universities and to descend to progressively more trivial levels of the educational process.

Colleges and universities are becoming aware of what sort of bedfellows bureaucrats truly are.

But mere words, no matter how eloquent, won't stop the tide of government regulation that, having engulfed other sectors of our society, threatens to flood institutions of higher learning. Prompt, constructive action is needed before it's too late.

The first step, as Richard Lyman argues in Chapter 3, is to increase our knowledge of current regulation and to explore possible alternatives. Only the academy has the resources to undertake studies of this sort. Given their stake in the outcome, academics must commit considerable resources to this study.

A second step involves politics. Government will respond to the public's desires and expectations, but only if citizens make their views known. Fortunately, colleges and universities are blessed with large, articulate, political constituencies—faculty, students, alumni, parents, and local community residents. Each can provide important support; they need only be asked. The responsibility for encouraging participation must fall on college and university administrators and trustees, and the participation should include increased activism in all aspects of political life. Academic representatives, especially administrators and faculty, must develop working relationships with elected officials through reciprocal visits and an ongoing dialogue. The nation's Capitol Hill and our fifty U.S. statehouses must become as familiar to college and university personnel as their libraries and classrooms if federal policies and programs are to help, rather than hinder, their institutions.

Nan Wells, Princeton University's director of government affairs and primary liaison to the world of Washington, has said,

> Members of Congress are interested in serving their constituencies. People in the agencies want to write good programs. When it comes to laws affecting higher education, they need our views if they're going to succeed.

She is right. I urge all members of the academic community to follow her lead.

Representatives of colleges and universities, working with interest groups such as labor, the clergy, business, and others, can significantly affect public policy: affirmative action, social security, energy-efficient standards, even occupational health and safety regulations, to name a few. The American Council of Education recently studied the cost of these programs. Six higher education institutions complying with twelve federally mandated social programs spent an average of $9.5 million, double the amount paid five years earlier. Not surprisingly, more than half of the funds went for social security. The experience of other sectors of our society, including business, is the same.

Beyond our common problems, however, it is critical that businessmen come to understand their stake in opposing excessive regulation *wherever it occurs*. In this connection, businessmen have an important responsibility to speak out, and to take a strong public stand against many regulations affecting colleges and universities. Most business opposition to regulation is on its own behalf, and its motives are often called into question. Here, however, businessmen have a rare opportunity to become central spokesmen in a policy debate of great importance to the entire country. The reason is that reducing regulatory pressures on colleges and universities will reduce the general government tendency to regulate. When businessmen speak for higher education, therefore, they will also be speaking for business.

Secretary of Health, Education, and Welfare Joseph A. Califano, Jr., recently warned against "domination of education by the federal government." And he said,

> If I have seen anything made plain in the last year and a half, it is that when programs and dollars multiply, bureaucracies and regulations multiply also; paperwork and reporting requirements multiply; the temptation to interfere, however well meaning, grows. And thus the danger grows that the job we are trying to do with our programs will, ironically, be made even more difficult by the unwieldy requirements and burdensome procedures that these programs bring.

It would be hard to find anyone in business today who would disagree with the secretary. It is becoming increasingly difficult to find anyone in higher education who would, either.

The challenge is clear: building on our common interests, we must work to curb the stream of regulation that has invaded our lives and strive to restore the liberties that have made our nation what it is today. We owe our children—our scholars of tomorrow—no less.

Robert S. Hatfield
Chairman and Chief Executive Officer,
The Continental Group, Inc.

New York, New York
June 1979

1

PAUL SEABURY

The Advent of the Academic Bureaucrats

Campus cooperation with the bureaucracy. Higher education in the United States and in Europe. Federal control of the environment of thought, and of the methods of academic choice. The power of funding: the university as a public utility. The hazards of the leveling process.

The nature of our times is such that surprises are no longer as surprising as they were. Some large surprises, however, come as camels on little cats' feet; we may take no notice of their surreptitious entry, and thus cannot appreciate them until they are ensconced in our tent. Our daily fare of media shocks dulls our appreciation of powerful tendencies beneath the surface of things.

This book deals with one such contingency which only recently was spotted by monitors of American higher education. Federal regulation of universities looms over the landscape of U.S. higher education. Barely a decade ago, it was scarcely recognized; today, those concerned about the future of universities in the United States see the relationship between the federal government and higher education as a profoundly disturbing and complex entanglement—so complex, in fact, that a battle-scarred administrator might wonder whether the entanglement has irrevocably altered the character of higher education.

I

In the 1950s the optimism of reformers of higher education in America about prospects for the envigoration and enlargement of higher education was such that even some of the most worldly-wise discounted the risks and dangers of federal influence. James Bryant Conant, former president of Harvard University, in 1949 took note of the dangers—only to dismiss them. "Federal control," he wrote, "is potentially far more dangerous than state control. Indeed, the dangers in this quarter loom so large in some people's minds that they are opposed to all Federal aid." Having said this, Conant (1949:190–91) proceeded to discount it:

> This attitude is one I understand but with which I heartily disagree; on the one hand it fails to appreciate the real need, and on the other is too defeatist about the nature of our democracy. Granted a sufficient number of wide-awake citizens with a *national* interest in public education to act as watch dogs on Congress, we need not be too apprehensive about educational bureaucracies or centralized control.

Conant's complacency was sustained, or rather, was conditioned by his insistence upon a basic principle for the governance of such aid. He continued:

Federal funds should flow to the *state* and be dispersed within the state by state authorities acting according to state law. If this principle is adhered to in any plan for Federal aid to schools, control from Washington by the most zealous bureaucrat will be almost impossible to achieve.

Fifteen years after Conant wrote these complacent assurances, the American Council on Education (1963) made virtually no reference to the problem of federal regulation.

In point of fact, a glimpse at the current regulatory state of things in higher education would suffice to show that nearly all the problems of federal regulation are of very recent origin. A cascade of congressional legislation and the consequent growth of a new managerial bureaucracy in Washington began in earnest in the early 1960s. *But* by then Conant's benign view of federal aid to higher education lay largely in ruins. The linkage between higher education and national educational authority was a direct one. Indeed, individual colleges and universities contributed greatly to the dynamics of the process by which they came to be tied, in an unequal one-to-one relationship, to a distant, benign, and powerful benefactor. That much of this passed relatively unnoticed by most occupants of the groves of academe at the time is understandable, for the camel of federal regulatory interference was entering the tent when campuses were in turmoil for quite different reasons. It is particularly ironic that many academics who now show dismay at the obvious loss of university autonomy were among those who welcomed the federal presence in the first place.

I thought it perhaps useful to write a short chapter of my own in which this current malaise may be seen in historical perspective. One overriding theme of this book is whether the changing patterns of control over university life and higher education in general represent a fundamental break with the American educational tradition. For this quiet and relatively unobserved revolution has been, in its essentials, over the question: who governs, and for what purposes?

II

In our modern world we are accustomed to see national "development" occur (or at least be attempted) in a centralized fashion, with plans, goals, and central funding. It is, therefore, hard to believe that U.S. higher education came to full flower before the second world war *without* any plan. While the idea of the American university began as a European transplant in the seventeenth century, by the twentieth century the reality of higher education in the United States was of such extraordinary scope and magnitude as to be almost incomprehensible to a European. In the year 1939, institutions of higher learning were scattered across the length and breadth of the United States, exhibiting an astonishing diversity as regards educational mission, size, mode of governance, and regional uniqueness. In that year, while only about 8 percent of American youth of what we now call "college age" were actually attending college, the sheer number of them exceeded the total number of university students in the rest of the Western world. A few venerable institutions, such as Harvard, were able to associate themselves with the older European centers of learning in that their historical origins were romantically obscured in time; but most colleges and universities were distinctly recent artifacts—most of them were established after the Civil War. In antebellum America before 1860 there was, in the Germanic sense, no U.S. university, even though far-sighted statesmen like Jefferson had tried to imagine what one should be like.

This burgeoning of higher education swept across the face of the North American continent as the frontier moved westward. It occurred with no conscious "public policy" intention and no central plan. The federal government, before 1939, played no role in this vast scheme. Where state governments did play a role, it was by no means comparable to the activities of autocratic European governments, such as those of Prussia or France, which viewed higher education as valuable to the interests of the state. The U.S. state college, where it emerged, was a response instead to widespread civic demand. Higher education was seen as necessary to the needs of a democratic society.

The characteristic American view, being democratic, stressed education; the European, being aristocratic, stressed learning. There is a neat distinction between the two, in that Americans emphasized the act of "leading out"—as Jefferson saw it, reaching into a democratic society to find the very best—while Europeans emphasized the goals of training professional servants of the state, and of advancing the quality of the sciences and arts.

Tocqueville, a prophetic observer, was astonished when he first visited the United States by a sharp contrast between American views and those conventionally entertained in the educated classes of Europe. The American faith in the beneficial character of universal public education particularly impressed him. In Europe, the established forces feared that the diffusion of learning would endanger the social order; there was virtual unanimity among Americans that it would strengthen social bonds. In a diary note entitled "Public Instruction," he wrote in 1831 (Pierson 1959:74):

> They all agree that the spreading of education, which is useful to all peoples, is an absolute necessity for a free people like theirs. . . . Thus the great expenditure of these states has been for institutions for the education of the people. . . . I don't yet know what is thought here of the inconvenience of a partial education, so great with us. However, it seems to me that the greatest arguments advanced in Europe against the excessive diffusion of education do not apply here.

Religious morale in particular, he thought, would not be much hurt by this tendency; there was no real hostility in the United States between religion and science. Nor should it be feared that the diffusion of education among ordinary people would result in frustration and social unrest. "Here," he wrote, "the resources presented by nature are still so far beyond the efforts of man to exhaust them that there is no moral energy or intellectual activity which does not find a ready outlet.'' What if Europeans feared for the safety of the state, once the common man became literate? What did that have to do with America? Where was the government?

> In the matter of administration, [he wrote his father,] this country seems to me fallen into the opposite excess from that of France. With us the government concerns itself with everything; [here] there is, or appears to be, no government. All the good in centralization seems to be as unknown as all the bad; no central idea seems to govern the movement of the machine. Thence a mass of general results denying enumeration.

Tocqueville and his companion, Beaumont, were particularly struck by the power of Puritan values as they affected American education. These already were attenuated and secularized; education would now ''make democracy work.'' The process by which this transpired was spontaneous.

> The general principle in the matter of public education [he wrote (Pierson 1959:293–94)] is that any one is free to found a public school and to direct it as he pleases. It's an industry like other industries, the *consumers* being the judges and the state taking no hand whatever. . . . You ask me if this unlimited liberty produces bad results. I believe it produces only good.

III

Tocqueville's impressions, while correct in general, were nevertheless devoid of particular important nuances which he, as imperfect prophet, was unable to foresee. In point of fact, the rivulets which were commencing to flow into the broader stream of U.S. higher education were by no means alike; they came from many distinctive sources, and gave the American ''system'' such diversity that James B. Conant (1949) noted, a century later, it ''must seem a chaotic nightmare to a foreign visitor.''

What is essential for us to recognize in this haphazard diversity is that virtually all U.S. institutions of higher learning planted across the continent had their roots in either local communities, religious orders, or churches. Jefferson's proposal, in 1801, to establish a *national* university in Washington proved to be stillborn—no Congress since has been willing to authorize one. Why, given the widespread American enthusiasm for education, was this so? The inescapable explanation was a widespread fear that such an institution, in a federal republic, might tower over U.S. public education, giving it a state character repugnant to American civic values.[1]

IV

This historic chaos of American higher education, when closely inspected, betrays more order than an outsider would perceive at first glance. In point of fact, the historic order-in-diversity was seen in a division between private and state-supported schools; between religious and secular ones; among institutions with distinctive ethnic or cultural foundations, men's and women's colleges, truly "national" institutions such as the University of California and Harvard, elitist institutions such as the Ivy League colleges, and so forth. Across the length and breadth of the land, many colleges came into being which never succeeded (some never even aspired) to escape from the parochial mission which their founders originally assigned them. Viewed by our contemporary liberal standards, it makes no sense to uniformly endow these early colleges with undeserved laurels. The power of the Congregational clergy over New England colleges, Henry Adams (1948:41) recalled, was crusty, minute, and inquisitory. Their power was not broken until the American Revolution, but such vigilant guardianship long continued in many American institutions, particularly in religious ones.

V

A competitive tension among American colleges and universities was both unavoidable and, on balance, probably considerably more creative than destructive. Lacking the hierarchical authority and state discipline which characterized European higher education, the U.S. system instead displayed an unresolved tension among three distinct kinds of "value perspectives": an eager populistic idea, that higher education was meant to advance the needs of developing communities and their children; a view that the institution, to advance learning, must be sheltered from the whims, foibles, or passions of society; and a particularly purist notion, entertained by individual scholars, that their own intellectual freedoms constituted the core value of the academic way of life. These three perspectives never have been harmonious; yet without each of them present in some mix, it is inconceivable that the American system of higher education ever could have attained its extraordinary excellence.

As in so many other matters in a free society, the touchpoint of tension came between those who contributed the resources to the institution and those who received them.

He who pays the piper at least sometimes calls the tune. Among those American academics who yearned for greater autonomy there was always a theoretical possibility: one way to escape the annoying controls and interference of legislatures and well-meaning wealthy private benefactors would be to pattern the university after the model of the private business firm. The only notable American educator to argue the case for doing so did not get very far with the idea. Francis Wayland, president of Brown University, in 1850 asked whether the time had not come "to inquire whether we cannot furnish an article for which the demand will be, at least, somewhat remunerative," by providing "the education desired by the people" and "adapting the article produced to the wants of the community." Concealed in this language was the proposal that Brown would gain its revenues chiefly from student tuition fees in much the same fashion that the Berlitz language schools do today. The "firm" thus would prosper or falter in the marketplace of competition with other schools. Wayland proposed moving from the frying pan into a fire, and it is understandable that few educators, and virtually no academics, embraced this novel scheme—which, at Brown, was briefly tried and abandoned. Since this line of action was so unattractive to scholars and administrators both, the dilemmas of living at the beck and call of donors, endowers, and the taxpayer were preferable to depending upon the fickle whims of consumers with cash in hand.

This being the case, the tension was between academic freedom (narrowly defined as the freedom of the scholar or groups of scholars to pursue lines of inquiry unfettered by outside controls) and institutional goals. Administrators, obligated to broad institutional values, well knew the problematic character of the university's relationship to "external realities"; their method of dealing with them not infrequently was regarded by purist scholars as opportunistic, and even as betrayal. As Laurence Veysey (1965:414) put it, the dilemma consisted in this: "To honor the institution was to betray the cause of free speech; to act upon that cause was to subvert the institution." There is an irony in all this, if one bears Tocqueville's standards in mind; the cause of academic freedom was typically upheld as a virtuous defense of virtue, but often it was obviously advanced as a buffer against an intolerant or overly zealous democracy.[2]

VI

The history of universities abounds in both horror stories and curiosities. In later life, the historian Frederick Jackson Turner remembered a time when "members of the Board of Regents of Wisconsin used to sit with a red pencil in consultation over the lists of books submitted by the professors, and strike out those that failed to please their fancy, with irreverent comments on 'fool professors''' (Veysey 1965:388–89).[3] But, more typically, the record would show that, by and large, external benefactors were as much moved by pride and support as they were by censoriousness. Boards of trustees, even in state universities, acted as much as protective buffers for the institutions as watchful agents, and could take pride in their universities' accomplishments. Quite probably, also, as much damage has been done to colleges and universities from internal abuses as from external interventions.

VII

Whatever can be said about the merits of such a diffuse system as the American one, it certainly can be argued that it permitted an extraordinary diversity of missions, traditions, and experiments. Perhaps even many of the most "backward," intellectually lethargic, colleges could deserve some credit for their modest contribution to the advancement of learning. But among the more lively and productive institutions, those which had become truly national or cosmopolitan in reputation, both competitive emulation and institutional individuality could conspire to enhance the vitality of the system as a whole. Widely differing patterns of student admissions, faculty recruitment, curricula, and professional standards of evaluation—all these features of the "system as a whole" were symptomatic of American life in general, and of the conditions of civic freedom. In its diversity, American higher education bore some congruence with the American economic system. James Bryant Conant (1956:35) observed that it was

> no coincidence that our economic way of life and our unique American tradition of education are found together. The internal development of this nation . . . has been bound up with the unfolding of a characteristic American point of view about schools, colleges and universities.

A distinctive feature within all the diversity of the system, nevertheless, was that it was informed by a meritocratic ideal of equal opportunity—a Jeffersonian ideal all along.

VIII

If one knew little of the contemporary reality of federal regulation of universities and imagined the problem abstractly, one might think it quite different from what it actually is. Both the history of state control of higher education in Europe and the grim reality of state domination in totalitarian countries have involved control of the content of academic research and teaching. In communist countries, it has meant policing of political activities and/or beliefs of members of the academic community. These dangers are the ones to which American scholars have been extremely alert. (Ironically, such threats to U.S. academic freedom recently have come not from the government, but from ideological zealots within the university. At the height of student disorders in the 1960s, one academic correctly pointed out that the university's defense system was like the British plan for defending Singapore in 1941—all the guns pointed in the wrong direction. The enemy came up from behind.) But the federal government thus far has shown little inclination to behave in this particular monitory way.* The problem is not so much Big Brother as a nagging, wealthy, mother-in-law, whose checkbook we are all too well aware of.

*A conspicuous exception to this, however, can be seen in attempts by federal agencies to police university research on human subjects. University compliance with such federal requirements has led to elaborate bureaucratic measures of review of scholars' research designs. At Berkeley in 1973, compliance regulations included a stipulation that human subjects—including whole classes of persons—should be shielded from researchers if the proposed research might damage their reputations. This requirement was rescinded; thus, it is actually possible for a scholar even to legally propose a critical study of federal regulators of universities!

The torrent of federal regulations, far from being direct infringements on scholarship and teaching, have been aimed mainly at the context rather than the content of research, learning, and teaching. Yet the regulatory web now is so comprehensive that it touches all levels of university existence, while rarely impinging directly upon classroom activity or upon the scholar in his study. This is not exactly the Orwellian horror scholars have feared. It is not thought control. It is the control of the environment of thought, and control of the means by which the thinkers will be chosen.

It is easy to discern the chief objects of the regulators. In general, all of the regulatory aims mandated by Congress or autonomously contrived by federal agencies, even in contravention to legislation ("affirmative action" comes to mind), at first glance are benign from any conceivable standpoint; they were so intended by those who devised them. Many of them are well within the historical mainstream of U.S. democratic aspirations for higher education.

The benign purposes divide roughly into four categories: equality, individual and group rights (the right to privacy, for instance), safety, and humane treatment of man and beast alike. Who in his right mind could possibly take issue, in the abstract, with such happy aims? Thus it has been that the university community, including administrators, have been loath to resist directly and openly each successive federal wave as it has risen.

Who would directly challenge the idea of safety and health? Of rights of officially designated categories of ethnic minorities? Of women? Of the halt and blind? Of the aged? And who condone the maltreatment of a monkey, dog, or cat?* It is when one sees the rules and regulations at work that their genial philosophical purposes appear, in the cold light of day, unbelievably costly, damaging to the operation

*One might have said that being against such things was like being against motherhood—but such is an obsolete cliché; now it would be like being against sisterhood.

of universities, and frequently bizarre. (At Berkeley, in compliance with federal regulations, air-conditioning units now are obligatory for dog and cat domiciles in laboratories—a federal "right" not yet extended to humans.)

IX

Someone has said that to understand the United States one must understand the way her people think about education. But to understand education in this country today, one must understand the way bureaucrats think about the United States. Federal administrators appear to regard the university as one sector on the battle line of a federal war against every conceivable social problem. Universities may prove more vulnerable to these intrusions than most business firms have been, simply because all really important universities—and most others—are now dependent for their survival upon unremitting government funding. As Clark Kerr has said, the American university is now a public utility. It also has become a national social laboratory.

In these matters as well as in those pertaining to a nation's power in world affairs, an analytic distinction can be drawn between capabilities and intentions. The federal government's *capability* to intrude itself into the most intimate aspects of university affairs was well developed before its grandiose social *intentions* came into play. This was so because the federal government—through a wide array of its agencies—commenced in the 1950s to be the chief endower of university research and educational programs and of student subsidies. The first sign of this new development actually dates to the mid-1940s, in the form of the GI Bill of Rights. Congress having determined that the twelve million veterans of the war were by virtue of that *entitled* to higher education, it was not a difficult step later to begin to think the previously unthinkable—that all high school graduates might be so entitled also.

In the instance of student loans, grants, and other subsidies, the relationship typically was between the individual student and the government—and thus, aside from the massive effect which enrollment increases had upon universities, the effect of such federal programs was indirect. Much more significant to our concern was the development of an unmediated relationship between federal agencies and individual institutions, as the former *contracted* with the latter to carry out specified tasks.

Here we come upon the clue, the very essence of our current concern: in the eyes of the federal government, the university became a *contractor*. It voluntarily entered into a relationship with the government indistinguishable from that of a firm which is hired by the government to provide some product or service. In a legal sense, it thus is no different from a firm chosen by the government to provide it with paper clips, bombers, or pesticides. University attorneys, at the beginning of this odd-couple relationship, might have taken notice of an interesting development in the industrial sector which had begun to develop during World War II: as contractor, the firm could be required to abide by government regulations affecting its internal procedures. Putting the matter bleakly, the federal government can terminate a contract if the contractor fails to comply with its regulations. Thus the industrial model has been employed by government agencies as the principal basis for contractual compliance with government directives. This has been an awkward but powerful weapon. The measure of federal power is the degree of the contractor's dependence upon the "buyer." The relationship is unequal. Probably very few university administrators, at the beginning, were perceptive enough to wonder at what point the pleasant experience of being a beneficiary of government largesse would be transformed into the *condition* of permanent dependence. Yet such is the condition of most universities today.

X

What are we to make of this new atmosphere for American higher education? Subsequent chapters in this book will view it from a variety of contemporary perspectives. I simply aim to place the problem in historical context by asking the question: in what ways do these extensive federal controls alter the historic character of American higher education? A few reflections are in order.

It is in the nature of the "rule of law" that it treat subjects equally and not make invidious distinctions. Thus as federal directives governing university policies multiply in meticulous detail, they apply equally to all affected institutions.[4] Clearly, considering the federal government's desire to evenhandedly pursue its social goals through institutions of higher learning, one effect of this is to gradually or even spasmodically obliterate the dynamic diversity of higher education in the United States.

There is an inexorable logic in this leveling process, which is especially troublesome when we consider that the effects of the regulatory process are felt uniformly in *all* institutions of higher learning which in any direct way receive federal aid—whether these are private or public, secular or religious, male or female, "national" or local. If distinctions among sexes are uniformly to be abolished, if all institutions are to be "quota-ed" with respect to student admissions and hiring, if all institutions are to be required to have uniform provisions to ensure the rights of the handicapped, if all are to be equally subject to strict regulations protecting the privacy of individuals, if all are to be subject to records inspection to ensure compliance with federal guidelines—it may then be expected that the burden of these regulations will fall most painfully upon those institutions with the least resources to devote to such purposes. But the most disturbing aspect to this powerful tendency may be seen in the obliteration of distinctions among institutions.

This is most poignantly to be regretted in the case of universities which historically have been informed by a corporate sense of mission. These have chiefly been the private colleges, but not exclusively so. It is hardly an exaggeration to remark that since the demoralizing events of the 1960s, the *raison d'être* of many colleges and universities has become, as William Buckley observed of Berkeley, "diffuse and inchoate." Is it really possible any longer to imagine—under the regime of federal occupation—that uniqueness long can prevail over compulsions of uniformity? Or that a significant line can continue to be drawn between public and private educational "facilities"? To be sure, a few Don Quixotes can be found on the landscape of American higher education—private institutions like Hillsdale College in Michigan—which staunchly resist receiving a single cent from the federal government, thus to escape its regulatory clutches. But it would be fanciful to assume that the example can be widely imitated.*

XI

A reflection is in order: as regulations work to obliterate corporate distinctiveness, custom, and diversity, universities may more and more be reduced to engines of contractual compliance. They internalize the cumbersome modes of bureaucratic behavior for which the federal government is the role model. Two investigators of the effects of regulation on

*Zealous opponents of federal affirmative action quota programs, who sought constitutional relief from them by urging strict compliance with the clear language of the Civil Rights Act (which *forbids* the kinds of discrimination now routinely enforced by federal authorities) may have overlooked the possibility that federal inspectors in the future conceivably can be as ruthless in policing compliance with the act as they now are in policing regulations which contravene it. Whichever way the "Bakke" issue is ultimately resolved, it can be assumed that the aggregate powers of federal authority will remain undiminished.

the University of California have formulated a disturbing iron law: federal laws breed regulations; federal laws and regulations breed state laws and regulations; federal and state laws and regulations breed university regulations; federal and state laws and regulations and university regulations breed campus regulations; all regulations breed reports; reports breed further reports; reports and regulations provide excellent evidence that one is doing something when one is not (Bowker and Morgan 1977:406). The regulatory habit, in short, becomes internalized and a way of life. World-weary businessmen may find it refreshing to observe, with *Schadenfreude,* their historic liberal intellectual adversaries now swinging in the breeze, victims of the same torment many of them once favored for U.S. corporations. The instinctive response to this might be the usual "It serves you right," but such is not constructive advice—an academic might respond, not very helpful advice. The once-private sector of American life, what remains of it, is—as Maxim Litvinov once said of "peace"—indivisible.

2

RICHARD W. LYMAN

Federal Regulation and Institutional Autonomy: A University President's View

The cost of regulation to campus life—OSHA and the NLRB. Control of medical education. The threat to the curricula. The loss of autonomy in faculty decisions. Affirmative action problems. A Department of Education? The need for self-regulation.

"Some problems are so complex that it takes high intelligence just to be undecided about them."

Laurence J. Peter (1979:221)

In January 1973, OSHA (the Occupational Safety and Health Administration) sent an investigator to spend fourteen days going over the physical plant of Stanford University in search of violations of the Occupational Safety and Health Act of 1970. It was our first experience of an OSHA site visit, and it was occasioned by the complaint of an employee about the amount of iron powder in the air around the metal cutoff saw that it was his job to operate.

The law requires that, in the event of an employee complaint, OSHA must respond within forty-eight hours by investigating on the site. Once there, the investigator undertook to survey the entire plant, not just the portion that was related to the originating complaint. Our investigator was thorough. About two months later the university received a citation listing a total of fifty-three violations. A couple of these were serious; in particular, standing water was found near a 14,000-volt electrical panel in the basement of the Student Union. University carpenters worked until midnight on the day this was discovered, putting in a false floor covered with rubber matting, so that the union could remain in operation. Most of the citations were of a minor nature, however, such as a lack of "No Smoking" signs in a paint shop, or the fact that some of our fire extinguishers were not colored red.

The most troublesome citation insisted that the university must build a standard railing all around the roof of its medical center (area: 197,102 square feet), at a cost estimated at $100,000. This was appealed, and subsequently modified. The university complied by relocating walkways and, where this was not feasible, by putting standard rails where walkways came within ten feet of the edge of the roof. A standard railing was also put around the sundeck area used by residents and interns near their living quarters.

As for the fire extinguishers, some were brought into compliance by being partially swaddled in red reflective tape, a small joke that may or may not have been appreciated in Washington.

It would certainly be an exaggeration to suggest that this episode constituted a threat to the integrity of the institution, and the vast majority of people at Stanford were wholly unaware that it had occurred. I cite it because, in several respects, it provides a good introduction to the subject of federal regulation of universities. Like most such regulation, OSHA's presence on campus does not directly affect the academic life of the institution—although the costs of compliance, of course, affect the financial support available for academic programs. As in the case of federal regulations requiring that all of the university's programs must be accessible to the handicapped, the government sets requirements which cost a lot to meet, but it seldom does much to help provide the money.[1]

Although OSHA's authority extended to private universities from the start—in contrast to many other systems of federal regulation—regulations were drawn up mainly with industry in mind. At first, this created some serious problems of applicability. Universities are not quite the uniquely subtle and complex organisms they like to consider themselves, but they do possess a good many characteristics that make regulations suitable to a steel mill not always relevant or appropriate. And even industry, of course, has found some of OSHA's more intricate exercises very burdensome.

Our subsequent experience with the agency has, on occasion, proven costly. In particular, we spent several hundred thousand dollars making alterations in a 7.5-mile system of steam tunnels, some of them dating back to the original construction of the university in the 1890s. Yet clearly there is no reason why colleges and universities should be singled out for immunity to this kind of inspection and control. And our experience since 1973 suggests that the agency has become more sophisticated and more aware of the ease with which it can overstep the line between what is reasonable and what is either nit-picking or onerous beyond any realistic estimate of the risks involved.

The Occupational Safety and Health Act preempted state industrial safety laws, but provided that states could take over the program. Cal-OSHA acquired this responsibility on 1 January 1974. Funding is now 50 percent federal and 50 percent state for compliance functions, and 90 percent federal, 10 percent state for consultation functions. Cal-OSHA has responded to industry complaints by creating an on-site consulting service that Stanford has used to its advantage on many occasions. In October 1978, OSHA withdrew about 10 percent of the word volume of its standards, including 607 general standards and 321 specialized rules. It is widely assumed that regulation, once introduced in some area of our institutional life, can only get worse—in the sense of becoming more burdensome and unreasonable—as time goes on and as the bureaucracy grows in size, complexity, and appetite. Our experience with OSHA suggests that such is not always the case.

At the same time, it is undeniable that the regulatory climate for universities has changed remarkably in a short span of years, and that, in sum, the changes have produced enormous increases in our costs, additions to our administrative staff, a boon to the paper industry of awesome proportions, and a source of friction and litigiousness which in itself constitutes a fairly heavy penalty for whatever improvements in our behavior as institutions the regulators have managed to generate. Seldom do university presidents congregate these days without their conversation turning to the latest skirmish with "the Feds"—the very term suggesting a relationship of diminished cordiality between the universities and the national government.

Since much regulation to which universities are now subject represents extensions from other sectors of national life, most of it does not directly affect teaching and scholarship. We are much more regulated around our periphery than in the heart of the enterprise. But encroachments can come in indirect ways. An example is the extension of the National Labor Relations Board's (NLRB) jurisdiction to private colleges and universities in 1970 (publicly supported institutions come under the labor laws of the several states).

NLRB AND LABOR RELATIONS

This extension had the immediate effect of making the development of collective bargaining much more likely throughout the university. Where nonprofessional personnel are concerned, the fact that the laws administered by the NLRB were designed for industry and not for higher education has not caused major difficulties, although some of the old sense of community is lost when the customary adversary roles and rhetoric of management and labor come to the campus.

But when faculty members have sought unionization, the confusion has been considerable. The law was not written with them in mind, and the NLRB's experience provides inadequate guidance. The question of whether faculty members are part of labor or part of management has been the most dramatic source of controversy, and the board's judgments in the matter have not been notable for their consistency over time. The very fact that the question can arise suggests some difficulty in adapting the trade union model to academic life. How the faculty of a major university would continue to control the curriculum, direct the research thrust, and set and enforce standards for appointment to its own ranks and for promotion to tenure, while engaging in collective bargaining with something now called "management"—this is no trivial question. Small wonder, perhaps, that unionization of faculty has yet to get a real foothold in such institutions.

But this may well change if inflation continues to erode the economic position of university teachers. And, given the way the NLRB works in establishing bargaining units, faculty members may one day find themselves in a union dominated by other professionals—librarians, research associates, parafaculty—even though the faculty as such continues to vote against such a change. Under such circumstances it is difficult to imagine that the faculty's approach to its rights and responsibilities—and, indeed, the whole academic context in which it works—will not be affected in significant ways. The example of school teachers is, perhaps, evidence enough. And it is not implausible to believe that university administrations will begin to act more and more like corporate management, with diminished access for faculty, and with much greater codification and bureaucratization of the ways things get done in an academic institution than anyone in a major university can readily imagine today.

Yet in extending the jurisdiction of the NLRB to academe, the government's intention was not to alter the fundamental nature of the academic profession, but simply to provide university employees with a set of rights long enjoyed by other kinds of employees of large organizations. The federal government, and particularly the Congress, has generally shown a commendable reluctance to try to run the academic programs of colleges and universities. True, curricula have been influenced by a variety of incentives from the federal government, ranging from the GI Bill of post–World War II days through the National Defense Education Acts, which, for a time, gave major encouragement to the development of foreign language study, to the various training programs and programs of fellowship support that helped universities in the 1960s to build what now appears to be excess capacity in their graduate schools. Agencies such as the National Science Foundation and the National Endowments for the Arts and Humanities have not only supported research in universities, but have funded educational programs of many kinds. University presidents spend very little time deploring these "intrusions." Quite the contrary. The complaints have come when one or another program of federal subventions dwindles or is terminated.

In one major segment of the university, however, the relationship between the federal carrot and the federal stick has begun to be more worrisome, not only intrinsically, but for what it may foreshadow for the future of the rest of the institution. I refer to medical education.[2]

STANFORD UNIVERSITY MEDICAL CENTER

It is easy to understand why the federal government has become more pervasively involved with the operation of university medical centers than with any other part of the institution. Problems of health care delivery are seen as urgently requiring attention. Congressional actions affecting medical schools, teaching hospitals, and clinics are intended more as attempts to come to grips with these intractable problems than as attempts to run the academic programs of the institutions themselves. Yet the effects on curriculum, admissions policies, financial aid to students, and indeed the entire management of academic health centers have been considerable.

Of course, the Stanford Medical School starts out sharing all of the obligations for accountability to federal regulators that the rest of the university has under such laws as the Social Security Act, the Employee Retirement Income Security Act (ERISA), the Fair Labor Standards Act, the Family Educational Rights and Privacy Act of 1974 (more often referred to as the Buckley Amendment, after the then junior senator from New York, ironically, an extreme conservative and supposed foe of government interference in private institutions), and the Civil Rights Act of 1964 and its numerous legislative and regulatory progeny. But in addition, the Stanford Medical School, like others in its category, is more heavily funded by federal dollars in relation to its total expenditures than any other part of the university. Research support from Washington alone runs to some $32 million per year. Currently, 45 percent of patients in the university-owned hospital are there under Medicare or Medi-Cal (partially funded by Medicaid, the federal program for the medically indigent). Half the student loan money, without which sustaining a diverse student body would be impossible, comes from Washington. And until now, at least, the medical school has been the beneficiary (if that is the right word—we shall have cause to question it in a moment) of direct institutional support in the form of "capitation money," available to those institutions that agreed to increase their entering class size under the Health Manpower Act of 1971. Nowhere else in the university is there a real analogy to this core support, essentially unrestricted as to the purposes for which it may be spent—and therefore readily adaptable to becoming a relied-upon portion of the operating budget of the school.

Bringing together, then, the extent of the medical center's dependence upon federal funding, the acuteness nationally of concern about such questions as oversupply of some medical specialties and undersupply of others, and the generally increased willingness of government to reach into institutions in both the public and private sectors in pursuit of this or that social goal, one has little basis for surprise at the extent of the federal impact on the life of the center. Indeed, it may be thought remarkable that the curriculum leading to the MD degree has not been the target of federal intervention.[3]

Through the National Health Service Corps scholarship program, the government has sought, by means of incentives, to remedy the physician shortage in rural and inner-city areas. To receive such a scholarship, a student must commit himself/herself to serve in such an area for one year after graduation for each year of scholarship support; the minimum number of years in service is two. The penalty for failing to perform such obligated service is three times the amount of the scholarship assistance. And in the Health Professions Educational Assistance Act of 1976, the Congress has sought to change the distribution of doctors by specialty, through outright control of the number of residencies in each. Because residents are not generally regarded as students, the direction of their studies away from surgery, for example, and into family practice may not be instantly recognizable as an intervention in the academic program of the school. Yet the distinction is, at best, a fragile one.

The power and occasional capriciousness of federal mandates can perhaps be best demonstrated by reference to a brief, traumatic episode at our university a couple of years back. Reimbursement under Medicare will obviously be unduly expensive to the taxpayer if all hospitals can get reimbursed at the rates of those in the parts of the country where incomes and the cost of living are highest. Some geographic discrimination is therefore unavoidable. The Stanford Medical Center suddenly found itself about to lose some $4 million per annum, however, when it was tied for reimbursement purposes to Santa Clara County, in which its buildings are located, instead of to San Mateo County, which begins 500 yards to the north. After tense negotiations and several shuttlings back and forth to Washington on the part of the dean and university attorneys, an exception was worked out that allowed us to continue being reimbursed at the higher level. But institutional survival achieved in this way begins to take on the uncomfortable overtones of *The Perils of Pauline*.

Much more could be said about the web of regulation already in existence for academic medical centers. I have not even mentioned such vast areas as federal and state licensing requirements, or the "thirty-two separate codes, each with its own machinery for enforcement, inspection and reporting" (Rosenzweig et al. 1977:4), with which the facilities department must cope. Clearly, life must be easier in other parts of the university.

CURRICULA REVIEW

And it is easier. But whether it will remain so is very much an open question. An incident that took place during the process of drawing up regulations to carry out the intentions of Title IX of the Education Amendments of 1972 comes to mind.

The purpose of Title IX was and is, of course, to eliminate discrimination by sex from academic institutions that have federally supported programs. In April 1974 we came across a truly startling passage in the long, complicated regulations then being drafted. Section 86.34 (c) would have required institutions of higher education to "establish and use internal procedures for reviewing curricula, designed both to ensure that they do not reflect discrimination on the basis of sex and to resolve complaints concerning allegations of such discrimination, pursuant to procedural standards to be prescribed by the Director of the Office of Civil Rights [OCR]" in the Department of Health, Education, and Welfare (HEW).

Despite the reference to "internal procedures" and the limitation of OCR's role to that of prescribing "procedural standards," we were shocked at the notion of such an attempt to police what is taught, read, and said in the classroom. The drafters did have the delicacy to refer to the First Amendment as a possible inhibiting force should the government go further than the proposed requirement. But it was not reassuring to have them conclude by inviting comment on "the appropriateness of including provisions [in the federal regulations] which specifically define discriminatory content of curricula or curricular materials."[4]

It was difficult to imagine the then Secretary of HEW, Caspar Weinberger, with his known concern for institutional autonomy and academic freedom, knowingly putting forth this proposal. So I wrote him on 8 April 1974 saying just that, and called his attention to what was being proposed and to the implications thereof.

This is not an instance in which an executive agency proposes to promulgate regulations pursuant to a legislative action which is clear, but of uncertain constitutionality. Quite the contrary, what adds to the breathtaking quality of the proposal is its bland admission that, "The legislative history of Title IX does not indicate the extent, if any, to which Congress intended that provision to operate in this area." In the context in which it appears this can only mean that there is not one scrap of evidence to suggest that Congress ever entertained such a notion.

Happily, before that month was over I heard back from Secretary Weinberger, thanking me for having brought the matter to his attention, and stating flatly that neither the proposal as written nor anything like it would receive his signature. I, in turn, thanked the staff members who had brought it to *my* attention.

An encouraging result? Yes, in a way, but also perhaps a harbinger of the future. If intrusions by Washington into the general curriculum of universities are to come, they will almost certainly be undertaken, as in this abortive instance, on behalf of some broad general principle with which it is difficult indeed to differ: colleges and universities ought not to teach their students to be sexist. They will also almost certainly come because of political pressure exerted by a well-organized interest group that has a clear objective in mind, and that is ready to urge that government move against a higher educational "system" that is more often than not a house divided and ill equipped to respond effectively in its own defense.

ACADEMIC SELF-DEFENSE

That defense will predictably be made more difficult because the main argument from our side has to be a plea on behalf of institutional autonomy, which can all too readily be made to look self-serving and arrogant. A powerful example, and one in which we did *not* emerge victorious, came with the passage in 1977 of a statute in California which effectively eliminates mandatory retirement of employees on grounds of age, thus going far beyond the federal statute, passed in the same year, which raised the retirement age from sixty-five to seventy.

The California bill was far advanced—without hearings or, indeed, any serious attempt to estimate the consequences of so sweeping a piece of social legislation—before such interested parties as higher educational institutions or the business community were even aware of its existence. Very late in the day, then, some institutions tried to stop the bill, or persuade the governor to veto it, if only to allow time to weigh its possible effects on affirmative action, on opportunities for the young—and especially for young scholars already feeling the ill effects of the so-called "Ph.D surplus"—and on the capacity of higher educational institutions to maintain their vitality in the face of so drastic a shift in the balance between young and old on their faculties.

Governor Brown's refusal to veto the legislation was accompanied by a statement that, whereas the letters he had received in support of the bill tended to come from individuals, those opposing it tended to be from "the universities, corporations and other holders of power. This is a classic case of gigantic institutions putting their own archaic and stereotyped work rules ahead of individual freedom" (*Sacramento Bee,* 17 September 1977).

It does not seem likely that there will develop any shortage of politicians who are prepared to respond in that fashion. What, then, can the universities do about the threat of many more such unconsidered (one cannot even say "ill-considered" in this instance) mandates, all issued in the name of freedom, equity, and justice, and all directed at institutions in an era in which there is widespread public mistrust of any organization larger than a barbershop quartet?

One might argue that higher education is to some extent crying "Wolf!"—given the fairly limited extent of government controls so far, at least when compared with most of the rest of the world. It is, of course, possible that we are somewhat overreacting to the great increases in expense associated with meeting new standards of accountability, plus such harassment as provided by the burden of paperwork and occasional bureaucratic tomfoolery. The balance of good and evil in the regulation we have now is extraordinarily difficult to cast up. Some efforts to estimate the added costs imposed on a given institution by government regulation have been made, but even the most approximate accuracy is extremely difficult in such matters. For example, it has been reliably reported that "estimates of the economic inefficiencies caused by surface transportation regulation range from a few hundred million dollars to $20 billion," while arguments rage as to whether the cost of federal oil regulation is $2 billion a year or $15 billion (see Noll in MacAvoy 1978:9–10). It is unlikely that estimates of such costs are any more reliable when they are incurred by decentralized institutions proverbially plagued with problems of joint costs, such as research universities.

Much the same thing must be said of the benefits of regulation. The single most prominent set of issues in government regulation of universities has involved affirmative action to increase the participation of disadvantaged minorities and of women throughout the institution. Accompanied, as they have been, by the threat of withholding millions of dollars of federal research support, efforts to enforce affirmative action standards and procedures against universities have generated enormous controversies.

AFFIRMATIVE ACTION

Some consider affirmative action a sham exercise, more productive of paper justifications than actual results. The statistics are, as usual, almost endlessly manipulable, and the glass is forever being perceived as either half-full or half-empty. Faculties, in particular, do not change composition quickly, and even the most earnest efforts are not likely to produce quick results. But it is difficult to ascertain whether any given effort has been of the "most earnest" quality.

On the other hand, many consider affirmative action to have been effective, but in a mischievous way, providing a cover for "reverse discrimination" and a consequent net increase in social tensions and conflict. Arguments over the difference, if any, between "goals" and "quotas," haggling over whether the Classics Department is short by one FTE (full-time equivalent) or by one and seven-eighths, and over whether the gap, whichever it is, shall be closed by 1980 or 1987, can readily bring the whole issue into disrepute.

For what it may be worth, I believe that federally enforced affirmative action was necessary, if the *de facto* exclusion of blacks and people with Hispanic surnames and American Indians from the higher reaches of American colleges and universities was to be ended. And I further believe that it has done more good than harm in the university I know best. But I have also seen that the benefits have been achieved at a very considerable cost in dollars, tempers, and distractions caused by unclear guidelines and inadequate statistics, overlapping jurisdictions, and sometimes excessively literal-minded interpretations of the rules. And, at that, we have been monitored by a regional office of HEW whose people have been, on the whole, reasonable, responsible, and ready to listen. Not every institution has been so fortunate. Tales of arbitrariness and of differing interpretations of the same regulations among regions and agencies are legion. Similarly uncertain results might be reported in other major areas to which the federal government has paid attention.

ACADEMIC REACTION

Yet, in a sense, a debate over specific costs and benefits is beside the point. So is the observation that universities in other countries are far more closely constrained by regulation than are we. Inevitably, we compare our present and prospective experience more with our own past than with the experience of other lands—and to the extent that we do make the latter kind of comparison, it increases our sense of foreboding, for we have so long been a fortunate exception to the world's rules. When our leaders tell us that we ought to have a separate Department of Education in Washington, because practically all other nations have Ministries of Education, those who know something of what life is generally like under such ministries are more likely to shudder than to be persuaded.

The trends seem ominous. Government continues to expand its activities even while echoing the public clamor over excessive government meddling and expense. That this is happening without much shaping from ideology may be the reverse of comforting, for it means that there is no well-developed rationale against which to measure specific regulatory initiatives, nothing more than a very general sort of egalitarianism, powerfully allied with the historic and profound American faith in natural rights and distrust of institutions, especially large ones.

Small wonder, then, if the universities' responses to the trend have been uneven, often uncertain, conflicting, and confused. It took a number of years for institutions and their leaders to realize that their old immunities were fast disappearing. Even now, the perception of what is going on is probably somewhat dulled by the fact that so much of the justification for the welfare state, including its regulatory aspects, was initially produced by members of university faculties. To this day, a majority of faculty members in the social sciences and humanities probably regard this creation as more akin to Pygmalion than to Frankenstein. Administrators are, naturally, more thoroughly aroused, and some are making speeches worthy of Al Smith and the Liberty League of the 1930s. Such rhetoric will probably prove just as ineffectual as the league's did.

At times, the universities have succeeded in stopping or undoing harmful things. When, as part of the Health Professions Educational Assistance Act of 1976, Congress imposed quotas of American transfer students from foreign medical schools as the condition for continuing to receive capitation support, and required that the quotas be filled by admitting applicants without regard for the institution's established admissions standards, there was not only outcry from most of the medical schools and their parent universities, but more than a dozen stated unequivocally that they would rather forego the much-needed funding than submit to this blatant intrusion upon their control of their own admissions process. In Stanford's case, this would have meant the loss of $410,000 in one year. This perhaps unprecedented willingness to put a loss of money where our mouths were may have been decisive; the offending proposal was quite drastically modified in the direction of restoring institutional autonomy. But it is ominous that so small a fraction of the country's hundred and twenty-five medical schools felt in a position to take this action. And it is difficult to take great encouragement from so hard-won a victory against so manifestly wrongheaded a piece of legislation. If, to stand a chance of winning, we are going to require that much of the right to be on our side, and that much determination, we can expect to do a lot of losing, for the issues are seldom that clear and the determination seldom easy to muster.

The universities and their associations in Washington often have missed crucial opportunities to stop troublesome measures at their onset. No one was ready to do battle against the Buckley Amendment until it was too late, and the same was true, as we have seen, in the case of mandatory retirement. We currently have the tragicomic example of the Ethics in Government Act, which seems to be telling most university people serving on leave of absence in the federal government that they had better return to their campuses by 1 July 1979 when the law takes effect, or face legal penalties for being employed by institutions that do business with the government agencies for which they worked.

Even when we have been alert, we have not always been united. In the matter of quotas for foreign medical school transfers, the Association of American Medical Colleges and the Association of American Universities did not manage to present a united front. Differences of opinion regarding the creation of a Department of Education have prevented any clear call to arms from higher education, despite widespread misgivings about the proposal. It is hardly surprising that so complex and varied an array of institutions has more difficulty getting together on an issue than does the dairy lobby or the National Rifle Association. But our disunity enables Congress to argue repeatedly that it cannot do what we want, if only because we cannot seem to decide what we want ourselves.

Some knowledgeable observers believe that the way to blunt the edge of the regulatory thrust is to adopt self-regulation on a massive scale. If we identify our own problems and then devise solutions that are tailored to university conditions and needs, we shall be able to tell the federal government, "See, it isn't necessary for you to work on the matter—we've solved it ourselves." Or so the argument goes. But this presents some significant difficulties. Even institutions of higher learning that are fairly similar to one another find it hard to arrive at a common position on issues. To hope that all of higher education will be able to agree on a system of self-regulation seems somewhat fanciful.

Secondly, much of the regulation to which universities are subject is not peculiar to them, and their efforts to regulate themselves—where higher education is but one among many interests involved—can hardly be expected to make much difference. There is also a distinct possibility that self-regulation may result, not in fending off more regulation by others, but in stimulating it. The threat of government intervention in the accreditation processes of higher education is an example of what can happen.

What, then, is there to do, other than wring our hands? I conclude with an admittedly modest list of suggestions, not for cure, but at least for symptomatic relief.

(1) We must learn how the system (or nonsystem) of establishing policy in this area works, and see to it that we have staff both on the campus and in the Washington-based educational associations who know what's going on, and who un-

derstand the mechanisms with which one must work to be successful in shaping issues and answers. The Washington associations, though stronger than they were a few years ago, still do not command great respect among experienced legislators and members of the executive branch for their effectiveness. And to this day it is surprising how many major universities have hardly anyone working for them full-time on government relations matters. We need not—nay, cannot—match the oil industry dollar for dollar and lobbyist for lobbyist. But we are not even close to the position of strength that ought to be attainable by a set of institutions as important to the nation's life as the universities.

(2) We ought to do with federal regulation what we generally do with problems: teach about it and do research on it. Of course, we do that now, but not enough, not well enough.

(3) We must learn to make alliances in politics. There are faint stirrings of greater cooperation between business and higher education. Such cooperation will not always be possible, nor in our interest. But we ought not to imagine that we can win many battles by being above them.

(4) We ought to avoid overreaction. A classic contemporary bad example is the thrashing about over Title IX and equity for women in intercollegiate athletics on the part of the National Collegiate Athletic Association (NCAA), which is still under the impression that it can gain exemption from the courts on the grounds that federal money, although assuredly going to its member institutions, is not going to the support of athletics. This has been shown to be a losing wicket in other instances, and the NCAA has lost the first round in court, but persists with all the prescience and subtlety of a gored bull. Universities for years tried to make the case for being treated as the exception to everything they did not like. They have done less of that lately, but the memory lingers on in Washington. Crying "Wolf!" can be counterproductive, even when there are real wolves all around.

(5) On the other hand, we ought not to assume that to propose a compromise is the right answer to every challenge. The incident of the attempted policing of the curriculum against sexist influences is a case in point; abolition was the right answer and the only acceptable one.

(6) We ought to try once in a while to look gift horses squarely in the mouth. Medical school capitation grants are probably doomed anyhow; neither in Congress nor in the administration do they have many friends. But we might learn from them a painful lesson: the closer the federal government gets to direct funding of the core of our activities, the greater the danger that we shall become inescapably dependent upon that support, in which case our capacity to fight back when the regulatory going gets rough will be minimal.

Despite the contemporary outcry over bloated bureaucracies and federal meddling (actually, it is often worse at state and local levels), we are not likely to see a latter-day Adam Smith arise to sweep away the twentieth-century mercantilists and restore our lost liberties. Some of these liberties were shams anyhow, as witness our erstwhile "freedom" to exclude blacks and browns from our ranks, or to confine women to a few so-called "helping professions." Others are unavoidably sacrificed to the complexities of a technologically advanced society, and to the difficulties that individual citizens genuinely have in protecting themselves against large, impersonal organizations.

We can, however, hope to equip ourselves to do better at the defense of our legitimate interests than we have been doing. And there is still time, for by and large the most important of those interests, having to do with academic freedom and control of the curriculum, have not yet been made the targets of direct attack. If and when such attacks come, we cannot expect others to save us. The responsibility and the opportunity will be ours alone.

3

CASPAR W. WEINBERGER

Regulating the Universities

Application of affirmative action regulations. The Philadelphia Plan and executive orders. Equal opportunity—with and without effort. Reverse discrimination. Government interference in administrative policies—Columbia, Harvard, UC. Reform efforts in Washington. Costs and burdens of government regulation.

Back in the days when the question of federal aid to colleges and universities was still a yes-or-no issue, opponents of the idea prophesied that money from Washington would inevitably bring about federal control. When Congress was considering the National Defense Education Act in 1958, Senator Barry Goldwater warned that, "If adopted, this legislation will mark the inception of aid, supervision, and ultimately control of education in this country by federal authorities.''

Few predictions have so thoroughly withstood the test of hindsight. Federal money has brought more burdensome controls over universities than even most conservatives had anticipated or feared. What was originally envisioned by most universities as agreeable patronage has degenerated into an adversary relationship. A few institutions have refused to bend to the federal will by declining federal aid—Brigham Young University, Hillsdale College, and Wabash College, for example. But most universities have accepted federal money, and then chafed at the consequences. In a full-page advertisement, the presidents of four universities in Washington, DC—American, Catholic, George Washington, and Georgetown—declared the need for independence from increasing federal control. The presidents of both Harvard and Yale warned their alumni and friends that, in its evolving form, federal patronage poses a serious threat to higher education, one of the most serious threats of the next several decades.

Although federal regulation takes a variety of forms—covering such diverse issues as pensions, laboratory safety, and environmental effluents—regulation of university admission policies and hiring practices, particularly in faculty employment, has stimulated the most controversy in recent years. The substantive problem is interesting and important for itself. But the problem of ''affirmative action'' in the universities is even more important as a case history in bureaucracy—especially the difficulties in controlling a bureaucracy determined to go its own way, defying a clear legislative intent.

LEGISLATIVE BACKGROUND

The origins of federal oversight of university hiring practices go back to the mid-1960s. Title VII of the Civil Rights Act of

1964 expressly forbids discrimination by employers on grounds of race, color, religion, and national origin, either in the form of preferential hiring or advancement, or in the form of differential compensation. Federal authority was extended through the enforcement language of the legislation:

> Each federal department and agency which is empowered to extend federal financial assistance to any program or activity . . . is authorized and directed to effectuate the provisions of Section 601 (on nondiscrimination) with respect to such program or activity by issuing rules, regulations, or orders.

Contracting institutions deemed negligent in complying with these provisions could be held ineligible for such contracts, or their existing contracts could be terminated. The first steps in implementing the new act were two executive orders of President Johnson: Executive Order No. 11246 (1965) and Executive Order No. 11375 (1967), which extended protection against discrimination because of sex, and stated that

> the contractor will not discriminate against any employee or applicant because of race, color, religion, sex, or national origin. The contractor will take *affirmative action* to ensure that employees are treated during employment without regard to their race, color, religion, sex, or national origin.

Thus, affirmative action was brought forth by executive order, even though Congress never specifically ordered it and no one ever really defined it. As a result, however, government administrators were able to punish colleges which did not comply with rules that would vary from time to time, and which had never been enacted.

While colleges and universities were subject to the general provisions of the Civil Rights Act of 1964 and to subsequent executive orders authorizing cancellation of federal contracts for noncompliance, the mechanical, statistical approach to determining violation of the laws dates from the Labor Department's 1968 regulations as applied to academic institutions. More detailed requirements—including the requirement of a written affirmative action program by each institution—were added by Revised Order No. 4 of 1971, which contains the crucial requirement that, to be "acceptable," an institution's affirmative action program must include an analysis of areas within which the contractor is "deficient in the utilization of minority groups and women," and must establish "goals and timetables" for increasing such "utilization" so as to remedy these "deficiencies." The difference between presumably illegal quotas and "goals and timetables" has always appeared to me to be too thin for the head of a pin, particularly when the threat is made that federal funds will be denied if "goals" are not met within the "timetables." This directive is now administered by HEW (Department of Health, Education, and Welfare) enforcement procedures applied to universities, through authority delegated by the Labor Department.

The important point is that the Civil Rights Act of 1964 did not require, or even contemplate, affirmative action. The legal authority for contract-compliance programs, of which affirmative action is a part, derives—as we have seen—from a series of executive orders and Labor Department orders stemming from the government's general power to establish conditions for federal contractors in the name of efficiency.

Because contract compliance rests on this independent authority, the government has been able to require all federal contractors to take affirmative action, whether or not any discrimination was proven against them. What affirmative action meant was not clear, however. President Johnson said that it included—but should not be limited to—affirmative steps in hiring, recruiting, advertising, training, and salary raises.

The Nixon administration took an important additional step in June 1969, when it announced the Philadelphia Plan, which for the first time included numerical hiring goals for minorities working in the construction trades in Philadelphia. This was, however, based on a clear-cut finding of past discrimination by Philadelphia construction unions. The Philadelphia Plan was followed by Order No. 4 in January 1970, and then by Revised Order No. 4 in December 1971, which no longer required that actual past discrimination had to be found as a prerequisite to affirmative action.

The revised order requires all federal contractors with more than fifty employees and more than $50,000 in federal contracts to submit a detailed affirmative action plan to the Office of Federal Contract Compliance as a condition for retaining federal contracts. These plans must consist of two main parts. The first is a survey of the contractor's current work force to determine whether the contractor is "underutilizing" women, blacks, persons with Spanish surnames, persons of Oriental ancestry, or American Indians in any of its job classifications.

A sex or race is said to be underutilized if it is employed in numbers significantly smaller than would be expected if the employer hired persons from the available work force in a random, nondiscriminatory way. Thus, if 30 percent of the qualified or readily qualifiable bricklayers in a particular metropolitan area are black, while only 5 percent of a contractor's bricklayers are black, that contractor would be underutilizing the work force of readily available black bricklayers by a factor of 25 percent.

If any such underutilization is discovered, the contractor then must establish goals by sex and race, indicating the number of persons in each category the contractor should be employing in each job classification, and stating a timetable for reaching that numerical goal. Unlike the situation in Title VII cases, these goals and timetables must be established to correct underutilization, *whether or not that underutilization results from intentional discrimination*. Failure to produce goals and timetables may mean cancellation of all federal contracts for the contractor.

All of this will clearly *cause* discrimination amongst the bricklayers in the above example. What it can do to our universities, which have vastly different problems than those who employ bricklayers, is far more serious.

Universities, for a variety of reasons, are extremely vulnerable to this novel form of federal interference. Federal outlays relating to higher education have risen from $500 million in 1950 to $12 billion in 1978. Individual institutions, notably great and distinguished ones, are extraordinarily dependent on continuing receipt of federal support. The threat of permanent disqualification, if consummated, could destroy our best universities' abilities to continue to serve the nation by furnishing the highest quality education for our future leadership, and much of the research on which the nation's continued greatness so largely depends.

The general principle of nondiscriminatory hiring provoked virtually no opposition within the universities. Indeed, it was supported as a cardinal principle of faith. But the subversion of that principle, directing affirmative steps to achieve exact statistical proportionate representation by race and sex—even in the absence of past discrimination—is far more controversial. By late 1971 something of a brushfire, fanned by HEW compliance officers working with missionary zeal, had spread through American higher education. It was caused by the demand that universities, as a cost of obtaining or retaining their federal contracts, establish and then achieve hiring goals based upon race and sex, with little or no regard to any other qualifications or to the individuals concerned.

THE CASE AGAINST AFFIRMATIVE ACTION

Because so many of the arguments in this emotionally charged field are *ad hominem* in the extreme, I think it appropriate to introduce here a short personal note. When I became Secretary of Health, Education, and Welfare early in 1973, I inherited an affirmative action program to which I was philosophically opposed. I was unable then or now to see how we would ever cure discrimination by ordering it to be practiced. The Office of Civil Rights at HEW, charged with enforcing affirmative action, was interpreting "equal opportunity" in a narrow, quantitative sense, hypnotized by the game of numbers. Its whole world was encompassed by statistics.

Equal opportunity, to me, means the right to compete equally for the rewards of excellence, not to share in its fruits regardless of personal effort. It was clear by 1973 that affirmative action meant inverse discrimination, and that it was jeopardizing a system that had allowed American higher education to develop and use the talents and excellence of all, no matter what their origins. Affirmative action, through a mixture of idealism, excessive zeal, and political anxiety, seemed to be destroying precisely those values which it had been brought into existence to protect.

But it was typical of the times that these views, whenever I expressed them, were attacked as "bigoted," "racist," and "sexist." Then—and now, to some extent—it seems impossible to have reasonable or rational debates on these subjects. I think my credentials as a believer in equal opportunity, and an advocate of it, were fully established. I had voted to establish a State Fair Employment Practices Commission while a California legislator in the early 1950s—long before it was fashionable. I had also worked at countless Republican gatherings to ensure that party platforms and resolutions firmly opposed racial discrimination and supported the principle of equal opportunity for all.

So I believed fully in these principles in 1973. I did not, however, believe that anyone should be pushed ahead by pushing others back. The first step clearly was to increase and improve the training of minorities, both in undergraduate and specialized graduate courses, so that we could continue to judge people on their qualifications for a particular job. I was very glad that this process was already underway. Black enrollments in colleges and graduate schools had been increasing rapidly. More and more women were going into occupational areas formerly considered reserved for males. Although these changes were not occurring as quickly as I would have liked, I did not believe that it was HEW's role to force colleges or universities to hire any but the most qualified applicant for the vacancy.

CIVIL RIGHTS AND REVERSE DISCRIMINATION

Before I became Secretary of HEW, the department had begun actively to enforce Revised Order No. 4, originally created to deal with racial bias in Philadelphia's construction unions, against institutions of higher education. A new form of racial discrimination had been imposed upon universities, not only with regard to faculty hiring, but also in student admissions. The former director of HEW's Office of Civil Rights had stated that universities could legitimately take race into account when choosing between two qualified job candidates in order to meet HEW's affirmative action goals. Indeed, it has become increasingly clear that not only would it be permissible for most universities to satisfy HEW discrimination, but it would be required of them.

According to four professors at Cornell, writing in the *New York Times* ("Letter to the Editor," 6 January 1972), deans and department chairmen had been informed by that university's president that HEW policy meant the "hiring of additional minority persons and females even if in many instances it may be necessary to hire unqualified or marginally qualified candidates." John H. Bunzel, president of California State College at San Jose in the early 1970s, recalls:

> I heard cases of people hiring someone just to avoid a hassle with the federal government. I know of people who received letters saying, "Your qualifications are excellent but we are looking for a black or a woman this year."

It is hard to say how widely such practices have been institutionalized in U.S. colleges and universities. But in 1973 the signs were troubling. In the preceding two years, increasing numbers of announcements for academic opportunities had made specific reference to the race, sex, or ethnic background of the prospective applicant, usually in such a way as to suggest that such applicants would receive preferential treatment. Samuel H. Solomon, special assistant in the

HEW Office of Civil Rights, had investigated seventy complaints of reverse discrimination, and had discovered that a number of colleges and universities were favoring women and minority candidates for faculty and staff jobs over equally qualified or better qualified white males. The implication was certain: large numbers of highly qualified scholars would pay with their careers simply because they were male and white, and our universities, on which so much of the nation's future leadership depends, would be gravely weakened—all because of the pursuit of statistical goals which disregard merit.

Excellent universities, which also happened to be those upon which the wrath of HEW's Office of Civil Rights had chiefly fallen before 1973, tend to recruit from other institutions of excellence. That is where they find the "skill pool" on which they rely. Paul Seabury (1972) described the problem as follows:

> If departments were to abandon the practice of looking to the best pools from which they could hope to draw, then quality would be seriously jeopardized. But to comply with HEW orders prior to 1973, departments could not hire the *best* candidate; rather they had to look for women or non-white candidates.
>
> For when a male or white candidate had been selected, it had become incumbent on both the department and university to *prove* that no qualified woman or non-white was found available. Some universities had already gone so far in emulating the federal bureaucracy as to have installed their own bureaucratic monitors, in the form of affirmative action coordinators, to screen recommendations for faculty appointments before final action was taken.

In the wake of the *Bakke* decision and its resulting ambiguities, it is still not clear whether such discrimination is legal in the narrowest sense. But it clearly violates the *spirit* of the 1964 Civil Rights Act, which mandated that each individual be judged on the basis of individual merit, not on the arbitrary basis of race, sex, age, religion, or national origin. Indeed, it was the fact that individuals *had* been judged on these irrelevant grounds that brought Title VII into existence.

To deny a person employment because he is white is just as wrong as to deny him employment because he is black.

Those in the Labor Department enforcing Title VII, however, had interpreted it to mean its opposite. They were not enforcing the law passed by the elected representatives of the people in Congress; instead, they were making a new law of their own. And HEW was required to adopt the Labor Department's regulations.

The problems extended beyond discriminatory consequences to extralegal procedural inequities. Properly, we put the burden of proof on the accuser, but this principle had been reversed by those administering affirmative action programs.

> To remain eligible for federal contacts . . . [Seabury (1972) writes] universities were forced to devise package proposals, containing stated targets for preferential hiring on grounds of race and sex. HEW could reject these goals, even though no direct charges of discrimination had been brought.

No proof—or even hard evidence—was necessary for the agency to conclude that the makeup of the academic population resulted from discrimination, rather than reflecting simply the general social conditions and makeup of qualified groups outside the institution. Yet when HEW found discrimination, based solely on statistical patterns, it could require that the university comply with abstract goals, regardless of individual merit.

These problems were particularly evident in November 1971, when HEW's Office for Civil Rights announced its intention to proceed against Columbia University, roughly half of whose annual budget came from the federal government. Without charges or findings of discrimination, Columbia faced permanent suspension of funds, because it had not come up with an acceptable affirmative action program to redress "inequities" which had not even been found to exist.

Although the Columbia incident occurred almost eighteen months before I began at HEW, it was not difficult for me to sympathize with university officials. Seventy-seven autonomous units generate proposals for faculty recruitment at Columbia. Faculty hiring procedures are decentralized; they devolve chiefly upon departments. Faculties resent—most of the time, quite properly—attempts of administrators to tell them whom to hire, and whom not. Departments rarely keep records of the communications and transactions which precede the extending of an employment offer, except as these records pertain to the individual finally selected. Even without affirmative action compliance requirements, the procedure is time-consuming and expensive. But Columbia's problem essentially was that it did not have the documents to prove it was innocent.

Another difficulty arose from the fact that most academic employment forms did not require racial information, both because laws in many states specifically forbade the practice, and because most colleges and universities—at least in recent years before affirmative action—have properly shown little interest in race or national origin when recruiting professors. After all, an argument that race is a proper factor to consider in hiring someone can only lead to the conclusion that race is also a proper factor to consider in *not* hiring somebody else.

As a result of this lack of data, the HEW Office of Civil Rights had forced a number of schools into such bizarre antics as judging racial or ethnic origin by analyzing the name or physical appearance of the professor.

But apart from methodological difficulties, a bottomless pit of complications, irrelevancies, and uncertainties results when categorical boundary lines are drawn and statistics generated, at a large cost of time and money. Statistical laws may apply to large numbers of random employees, but universities do not hire large numbers of random academic employees; they hire small numbers of specialists.

Nowhere can one observe random distribution of those interests and talents vital to any great university. But the government's standard, approved, affirmative action programs implicitly assume such a distribution. Neither minorities nor women are randomly distributed by field or within fields. A law school is not looking simply for a brilliant legal scholar; it may be looking for an international tax expert, or a practicing lawyer who can teach both an advanced seminar on the Uniform Commercial Code and a first-year class on contracts. Even if categories could be meaningfully drawn—which they usually cannot—the necessary statistics as to how many of these hybrids were white, black, or yellow would almost certainly be unavailable. And even if categories could be defined and statistics somehow generated, there is no reason to suppose that fair processes in individual cases would automatically produce results demanded by the timetables and statistical goals that HEW required them to develop.

BUREAUCRATIC OBSTACLES TO REFORM

Being aware of problems and dangers related to affirmative action is one thing; doing something about them is quite another. One would think that the most obvious and effective thing to do would be to appoint subordinates who would help change department policy. The difficulties in accomplishing this may be appreciated from a glance at Figure 1, which reveals the immensity of the bureaucratic and organizational problem. With a total annual budget exceeding $150 billion, the Secretary of HEW has responsibility for administering some 350 separate programs. Civil rights compliance is conducted out of HEW's nine regional offices. These are run by regional directors, each of whom is responsible for administering more than 100 programs which employ thousands of persons—11,000 in the San Francisco regional office alone.

In this setting, the appointment authority of the Secretary of HEW extends to only a few top positions—in 1973, fewer than one hundred in an agency of 148,000 people. Moreover, the Civil Service laws, emphasizing merit, have made it virtually impossible to discharge or replace anyone for any reason other than the most serious cause—and then only after lengthy hearings and appeals that generally outlast even comparatively long-surviving appointees. Thus, the great bulk of the people engaged in any department administrative activity will have been there over a long period. Bureaucratic tenure is not necessarily fatal to attempts to change policy.

I have found in all my government assignments that most permanent Civil Service employees at federal, state, and local levels are loyal, dedicated, and generally able people who will accept and implement policies—and changes in policies—determined by appointed officials. But there are exceptions. There are some who oppose policies so fiercely that they will try to avoid implementing them, and will even try to undermine them by leaks to friends in the press or on Capitol Hill. Despite such opposition, the reservoir of loyal employees is usually large enough to allow new policies to get a start. It is also possible to establish procedures which force decisions from tenured officials.

It is far easier, of course, for appointed policymaking officers to accept and follow staff recommendations; that is why policies of major departments seem to change so seldom, no matter who is in office. It is more difficult, but more rewarding, to establish policy yardsticks which allow judgment of whether staff recommendations are in accordance with a previously determined policy. In this case, quite a lot can be accomplished.

Establishing policy, however, is only the beginning of the problem. In an agency as large as HEW, with its then 148,000 employees, it is difficult to know how many—and who among them—are carrying out the new policies, particularly if these policies constitute a substantial reversal of past activities.

Thus, for example, I first learned of the actions of the Office of Civil Rights personnel in our Boston regional office when I received a telephone call from Harvard University President Derek Bok asking me if I knew that our people were telling him that the next vacancy in Harvard's History Department had to be a woman. His point was that the next vacancy in the Harvard History Department would occur when one of the world's leading authorities on Chinese history retired some two years from then. He was not at all sure that one of the world's leading authorities on Chinese history at that time would be a woman.

I assured him that I would never sign any orders denying Harvard federal funds for his failure to appoint a woman to that position unless Harvard did, indeed, refuse to appoint *the most qualified* person to teach Chinese history *because she was a woman*. Similarly, I could—and did—advise the director of the Office of Civil Rights, who was my appointee, that any orders denying federal funds to any universities would have to be reviewed personally by me, and that any recommendations to that end must be fully substantiated in files that I would read before any such decision was made.

I had even more disturbing reports from the chancellor of one major upstate New York university relating to the prosecutorial treatment of his university administrative people by several younger employees of the regional office of HEW. The incident occurred during attempts to secure what they felt were the required data on which to base required goals and timetables. This was corrected by calls to the regional office director.

The change in philosophy and policy were also communicated in other ways. During this period, in meetings with various civil rights, religious, and other groups, I gave frank statements of my own views on the subject; especially of my strong feeling that, in our blind pursuit of statistical goals, we were forgetting about merit as a basis for appointment. I often argued that even if we achieved, in the microcosm of a university faculty, the perfect mirroring of the ethnic composition of any given neighborhood at any one time, we would have accomplished nothing useful or effective in assuring academic quality or faculty usefulness to students. These meetings frequently resulted in angry and bewildered responses from attendees who could not understand how anyone could challenge the perfect wisdom of the numbers game

they were playing. But they reported the results to others within the department. By this means, as well as through the regular and frequent staff meetings, the philosophy and change of policy were signaled.

On at least two occasions, I refused to follow recommendations for termination of federal funding for the University of California. I called its then President Charles Hitch, advising him of problems our people had with the university's affirmative action plan, and of my feeling that the university could establish its good faith in hiring practices and promotion, so to avoid the penalty of loss of federal funds. A solution was thus accomplished sooner and more effectively than if the department had suddenly withdrawn all federal funding, had brought some of the university's vital research efforts to a halt, and had deprived thousands of students of the opportunity to continue their education at one of the world's great institutions.

Essentially, the approved plan requires that over the next thirty years the universities will fill many posts with *qualified* women and minorities, as they become available. For this I cheerfully accepted various harsh criticisms, including being picketed by a women's group before and after talks in San Francisco. Besides the pickets, criticism included editorials and outraged statements by attorneys paid to represent civil rights groups at meetings. After a few such meetings in which I held my position firmly, they took their case to congressional committees and staff people in hopes of persuading us to return to past policies.

Such pressures are normally enough to prevent changes of policy. However, my belief was that affirmative action, as demanded, would undermine the quality of the universities, and would also subvert the actual and worthy intent of the civil rights acts. By adhering firmly to my beliefs, I was able to bring about some changes in course—and at least prevent imposition of the ultimate penalties sought by vigorous opponents. I responded to congressional critics that if they wanted to cut off a university's funds because its faculty did not mirror the ethnic breakdown of the surrounding community, without regard to other qualities, they would have to say so specifically by statute, and they had not yet done that.

I also instituted—without success—a major effort to change the Department of Labor's regulations, which applied to HEW's administration of Federal Aid to Education. Conversation with Secretary of Labor John Dunlop produced general, verbal agreement. But he reported (and apparently concluded) that his own bureaucracy would be outraged by any major change in policy, so we were left with regulations which prescribed strict numerical goals, timetables, and (I felt) illegal quotas.

None of this should imply that there was any attempt to violate these regulations or the law, which, I felt strongly, did not require regulations of this type. My policy at HEW did mean, however, that universities were not deprived of federal funds simply because they did not produce the reams of statistical material demanded within thirty days by some permanent department employees, and it meant that universities did not lose federal funds simply because they failed to meet timetables for preferential and inversely discriminatory hiring.

Despite criticisms from individual congressmen and their staff members, I was encouraged that Congress never changed the basic law to require the inverse discrimination which the existing regulations seemed to require. I was also encouraged by the fact that I was never ordered by either President Nixon or President Ford to change these policies, nor to set HEW back on the paths it formerly followed.

IMPACT ON THE UNIVERSITIES AND CONTROL OF THE BUREAUCRACY

All of the foregoing problems with affirmative action—its discriminatory effects, its procedural inequities, its misconceptions—could have been foreseen. What I had not fully anticipated, however, were the administrative costs and burdens imposed on colleges by the program; nor the fierceness with which these statistical absurdities were used by some of those charged with enforcing what had now become the law without benefit of congressional enactment.

Colleges and universities are not strangers to bureaucracy, but the new laws created a large corps of instant Jeffersonians. Schools attempting to comply with affirmative action programming found themselves trapped in a mass of paperwork, a labyrinth of bureaucratic guidelines, and an endlessly conflicting collection of definitions concerning "good faith," "equity," "minorities," "goals," and "quotas."

College and university officials found it especially difficult to establish satisfactory working relationships with HEW enforcement personnel. Critics charged that the HEW regulators were uninformed about the educational process; that they required the gathering of useless data, caused long and inexplicable delays, and played "cat and mouse" games over enforcement.

Whether or not these charges were correct, the sheer volume of resources required to gather and process data, to write huge reports (typically weighing several pounds), and to conduct interminable communications with federal officials was staggering. It took the University of California over a year to prepare the mountain of paperwork that affirmative action reports required, including some 70,000 to 80,000 statistical calculations. Such useless tasks were imposed on universities that were guilty of nothing, and against which no legal sanctions had even been imposed. Although no one knows the exact costs, the waste involved and diversion of resources was best expressed at Senate subcommittee hearings on the issue, where one college president testified, "Every time I have to hire a lawyer, I have to turn down an appointment of one Associate Professor."

An important but indirect cost of the increased paperwork accompanying affirmative action was its impact on the atmosphere in which important decisions were made. The entire academic hiring process became slower, more laborious, more costly, and less certain. These changes also had important implications for departmental autonomy in universities. UCLA economist Thomas Sowell (1975) stresses this point:

> Faculty decision making on hiring, pay, and promotion is increasingly being superseded by administrative determination, in response to affirmative action pressures on academic institutions. The historic informal balance of power is being shifted away from those with specific expertise in their fields to those who feel outside pressures to generate either acceptable numbers or acceptable procedures, excuses, or promises. The bitterness and demoralization generated by this undermining of traditional faculty autonomy occurs whether or not any minority or female faculty members are eventually hired.

But the saddening cost of affirmative action is the special damage which it inflicts upon the very people for whose benefit the program presumably operates. The hiring of professors or admission of students on any basis other than ability works a particular hardship on the "favored" groups. Young minority and female scholars must now enter an academic world where they face resentment, doubt, and presumptions of incompetence. The appearance of massive benefits being conferred on minorities and women undermines the very real achievements of minorities and women themselves—achievements whose general recognition would be a very healthy influence on society at large. In Sowell's words, "that bitterness not only has been directed against those administering affirmative action programs, but has inevitably affected the perception and reception of minorities and women in the academic world—and beyond."

In considering solutions to these very real and continuing problems, I am struck by the major effort that is required to bring about even minimal improvement, once a policy starts moving down a particular path.

We have seen the dangers inherent in affirmative action as imposed on our universities. We have seen that nothing in the law requires us to try to cure discrimination by ordering another kind of discrimination to be practiced. We have seen that policy repeatedly carried out by departments whose leaders either favored it or were afraid to fight it. So far as I know, I was the only HEW Secretary to oppose this version of affirmative action. While I was able to reverse the policy in a significant number of individual cases, it is apparent that unless the courts, Congress, or the president, by use of his appointive power, intervene to change matters, universities will continue to be subjected to the heavy, costly, and irreparably damaging burden of being required, without statutory authorization, to disregard merit in faculty appointments and promotions and in student admissions.

The courts could solve the problem if they would deliver clear-cut opinions forbidding the practice of *any* discrimination against anyone in these cases. The Congress could solve it, if by statute it would clearly forbid any suggestion of penalties against a university whose appointment, admission, and promotion policies were based on merit. The president could solve it if he would require his appointees to insist that all threats of withholding federal funds against universities which use merit as the test be withdrawn, and if he would insist on regular reports from his appointees demonstrating that his policies were being honored.

Otherwise we will have to rely on the occasional appointment to high position of someone who feels sufficiently strongly about the issue to ignore constant criticism, as minority lobbies seek to preserve an administrative victory won without benefit of congressional enactment or endorsement at the polls. The average tenure of secretaries of HEW, for example, is about eleven to thirteen months; thus, if we are relegated to waiting for an opponent of affirmative action to be named, it may be a long time before we will see any permanent change in this pernicious policy. To change a major policy of this type, we must try to secure the election of a president who is not content with trying to placate all—by refusing to stray from the ambiguous middle and by skillful use of whatever rhetoric seems required by the polls, but whose actions never match his rhetoric.

And even if the president has the courage to appoint cabinet members who are not afraid to take firm and effective stands against this type of affirmative action, those cabinet members, in turn, must establish close and continuing surveillance of their own appointees and of career officers charged with carrying out policy to make certain that *their* policies are, in fact, being carried out.

Only then could we have any confidence that excellence would again be the guiding principle in the appointment and promotion of faculty members and in the admission of students.

CONCLUSION

Justice Louis Brandeis once said,

> Experience should teach us to be most on our guard to protect liberty when the government's purposes are beneficent. The greatest dangers to liberty lurk in insidious encroachment by means of zeal, well-meaning but without understanding.

Our experience with affirmative action in higher education corroborates this observation.

But an important and more general lesson would be lost if we thought that the federal government made a unique kind of error when it undertook to regulate university hiring practices. Universities are not necessarily more complex than other private institutions—corporations, hospitals, private foundations, and the like—or so different that regulation would be uniquely destructive when applied to them. Universities have many unique features, but they share many qualities with other members of the economic marketplace. The case against politicization of universities is no stronger than the case against politicization of other private organizations and institutions. There is no reason to believe that the bureaucratic single-mindedness and procedural inequities which accompany affirmative action regulation in higher education are any more excessive or uncontrollable than those which accompany regulation in other parts of the economy. Government regulation that attempts to cure discrimination by practicing it is equally bad in a university or in a glove factory.

What we are witnessing now—affirmative action is but one example—is a political phenomenon in which government regulation expands to control the decision-making processes of private institutions. The claims and expectations of government with respect to all institutions, of which universities are one form, reflect an increasingly simplistic view of society's possibilities for improvement, and a growing belief that government action can guarantee fairness in every relationship. The dominant peril of our time, and of the decades ahead, is that we have failed to understand the dangers to human liberties in our continually increasing use of government.

It is ironic that the academic community, which has justifiably recoiled from government regulation in its own sphere, has strongly tended to support this political control of the other institutions of our society.

> The result [as former Solicitor General Robert Bork points out] is not only that many today take pleasure in the plight of academics forced to swallow their own medicine, but also that the public philosophy of dispersed authority has been undermined and ridiculed by intellectuals who now invoke it for their own benefit.

One possible dividend of the affirmative action controversy is that it may have provided academicians with a firsthand glimpse into the nature of bureaucratic government. Given the vital role academic intellectuals play in forming political and economic ideas, it is essential for them to realize that the bureaucratic flaws revealed in affirmative action compliance programs—overzealousness, unevenness, capriciousness, and arbitrary actions—are endemic to the regulatory mode of behavior. These imperatives stem from our tendency to create a new bureaucracy every time we find a new principle or goal some group wishes to achieve, or even when we encounter what some special interest group calls a problem.

Ultimately, the health of our universities will be determined by the health of our society's other nongovernmental institutions. Many in the academic world have been actively hostile to the claims of those other organizations. This leads me to agree with Robert Bork's suggestion that "the fate of the universities ultimately depends on whether the large intellectual group they house comes to understand the institutions of our society or continues to press for statist, central control in all areas but their own."

Perhaps even more than the fate of our universities, our own future as a nation is involved. And that, I believe, can only be secure if our universities constantly and unremittingly pursue the goals of excellence and truth. And they can never do that if they are required by those in fear of minority lobbyists to subordinate excellence to narrow statistical goals in pursuit of unenacted versions of affirmative action.

4

ROBERT L. SPROULL

Federal Regulation and the Natural Sciences

Government research contracts and their controls. The investigator. Fiscal intervention; audits. Agencies in the laboratory. The effect of red tape on scientific flexibility. The Ph.D. glut. Scare tactics and public speculation. Health and safety regulations. Patents. University/industry cooperative research.

I

The natural sciences have flourished to an unprecedented extent in the third of a century since World War II. Medical scientists have conquered poliomyelitis and eradicated smallpox. Biochemists have worked out the structure of DNA and linked their new understanding of genetic material to development and disease. Geologists, through the theory of plate tectonics, have demonstrated motions of the earth's crust that are global in scale and awesome in implications. Chemists have developed spectacular new materials, drugs, and understanding of molecular processes. Physicists have discovered a host of fascinating phenomena in condensed matter, and a bestiary of subatomic particles that defy the imagination. Scientists have moved substantially closer to answering the ultimate question of the origin of the universe. Applied science in solid-state devices and inertial guidance has made space travel possible and given mankind, for the first time, the ability to see his earthly home from a distance.

In the United States, where the great majority of these golden age discoveries have occurred, the federal government has been the most pervasive influence and the single most consequential element in the development. Yet American scientists now look, nearly unanimously, with jaundiced eyes on the federal role. Formerly partners in an undertaking viewed as important by both, the government and the universities now face each other with suspicion or even antagonism.

Part of the reason for the deterioration of relations originates from direct federal regulation of research in the natural sciences, a topic which we shall address in section III. This regulation is largely similar to the regulation of industry and of citizens' activities in general. An even more consequential federal regulation of the natural sciences has developed indirectly, in the policies and practices for the federal support of scientific research. It is this indirect regulation that hurts research most, and we address it next.

II

Two basic decisions of 1945–1946 still profoundly shape the natural sciences in America. The first was that substantial federal funds would be injected into scientific research, initially through "mission" agencies like the Office of Naval Research (ONR), and later also through the National Science Foundation (NSF). The second was that nearly all of the support of basic science (and much of applied science) would be in institutions (research universities) where research was intimately related to advanced education. Both policies originated in the spectacular success of applied science in World War II: microwave radar, nuclear weapons, proximity fuses, operations research, synthetic chemistry, and many others. In all of these developments, university scientists and their students, converted for the emergency, augmented the forces of scientists and engineers in industry. If the nation was to retain the ability for similar developments in peacetime and in preparation for future emergencies, the lesson was clear: support the natural sciences, and support them in such a way that new generations of advanced students are prepared, using modern research equipment and in close contact with the research frontier.

Both of these major policies are, in a sense, invisible. There is now no one who is a principal investigator in a U.S. university who played a similar role in a prewar university; we have all forgotten that (with the exception of the Department of Agriculture and some tiny contracts from the Army Signal Corps and a few other agencies) there was no government support of external research before 1939. Similarly, we have all grown up on the postwar American pattern, and we tend to ignore the possibility of the separation of advanced training from government-supported research; the pattern in the USSR is quite different, with research institutes separate from the universities. As a result, the USSR must overwhelm a research problem by applying large numbers of people, since neither the research institutes nor the universities rival U.S. institutions in quality.

The Office of Naval Research established the powerful traditions that have served science and the nation well. Program managers in Washington were themselves scientists. Some of them would go on leave for a few months or a year as active participants in university research; professors would serve in ONR for a year or two as program managers. Promising individuals were supported, even if the possible connection of their research to navy problems was tenuous at best. Self-restraint was exercised in terminating contracts; although the contract instrument usually specified one-year support (in later years this often grew to two or three years), a principal investigator could plan research in the confidence of five- to ten-year continuity. The universities were willing to expand professorial staffs, including tenured faculty, and to build and assign prime space on their campuses because of this continuity. The navy benefited by interesting the able investigators ONR supported in navy missions and problems, and by the expansion of the scientific and technological base of the country. The ONR and the universities constituted a partnership with positive advantages for both; it was *more* than a zero-sum game.

Other agencies were created in the ONR tradition; indeed, many were initiated by transferring key people from ONR or its contractors. The Atomic Energy Commission (AEC) began research contracting with policies even more long-range and farsighted. The explosive expansion of the National Institutes of Health (NIH) and the creation of the National Science Foundation broadened and intensified federal support. The Army Research Office (ARO), the Air Force Office of Scientific Research (AFOSR), the Advanced Research Projects Agency (ARPA), and other defense agencies complemented ONR in the defense mission; the National Aeronautics and Space Administration (NASA) further broadened federal research support.

Two examples from the 1945–1955 era illustrate the success of the new approach. ONR provided the equipment and initial research funding to permit a score or more of university laboratories to work with liquid helium. At that time, such work at ultralow temperatures (within a few degrees of the absolute zero of temperature, minus 460° F) was considered very "far out." The developments in solid-state physics, chemistry, and technology that have flowed from this modest investment have enormously strengthened the nation.

The second example is even more obvious. William Shockley and his colleagues at Bell Telephone Laboratories (BTL) invented the transistor and the understanding of electronic processes in semiconductors which have led to the huge industry of solid-state devices and the large-scale computers, communication systems, and information systems based on them. ONR, AEC, ARO, AFOSR, and other federal agencies had been sponsoring work in semiconductors and related fields and in mathematics. The development from the *invention* to the *industry* proceeded extremely rapidly in the United States because of the people with advanced training supported by these agencies. This is not to take away anything from the foresight of BTL, IBM, and other corporations; but, in addition to their imagination and judgment, these corporations enjoyed the availability of trained manpower that was one of the earliest and greatest successes of the ONR tradition. The "edge" of the United States over Japan and the European nations in the computer industry owes much to the federal agencies.

Regulation accompanied this support, but the regulation did not intrude into the research conception or effectiveness. Of course, government auditors had to be satisfied, but they were properly concerned with possible misuse of funds, not with managing the research. There was an occasional skirmish over threats to classify individual research projects, but secrecy was very rarely imposed. Relations between a principal investigator and the agency that sponsored his work were invariably cordial, and the investigator usually served the agency and the government in other ways, mostly informally and without compensation.

This cooperative era has now given way to much less productive relations, involving more federal regulation and control, micromanagement from Washington, less research and less imaginative research per federal dollar, and a "we/they" tension between the bench scientist and his Washington counterpart.

The most intrusive regulation is fiscal. An investigator proposes a piece of research; the award of a grant is made largely on the basis of the reputation and promise of the investigator, but also partly on the basis of the "setting" of the proposed work within his university, the university's pool of equipment and facilities that will be available to him, and its "track record" of fiscal and managerial responsibility. The federal purpose would then best be served by leaving the investigator alone to pursue his ideas wherever his imagination and the imagination of his students and colleagues take him.

But this is not what happens. There is an inverted pyramid of inspectors to make certain that every tiny detail of the grant language is followed literally. The investigator keeps his own bookkeeping to determine what he can and cannot afford; this used to be by his own notes on the backs of used envelopes, but is now more likely to consume the time and cost of an administrative assistant. He is usually helped by a contract and grant office at his university; people in this office remind him of the paper pitfalls in grant language, help him to avoid disallowances (expenditures that advance the research, perhaps more efficiently than permitted expenditures, but for which the grant will not pay), and help him generate the paper for the renewal application (which sometimes must be put in motion at about the same time the work begins). Although the investigator and this group are "on the same side," the thicket of federal regulations is so complicated and forbidding that he sometimes looks upon the university's grant office, which helps him keep his bearings, as the generator of the problems.

The first layer of auditing overlayed on this management is made up of the internal auditors of the university. They verify that funds intended for a spectrophotometer were not used to buy a lawnmower, and assure themselves that accounting systems and controls are effective. The second layer is that of the public auditors of the university, who look over the shoulders of the internal officers, and who eventually bless the annual financial statements of the university with language like "accepted accounting practices."

The third layer is the federal resident auditors. Typically, these are employed by the Department of Health, Education, and Welfare (HEW), but at some institutions the Defense Contract Audit Agency (DCAA) serves. These auditors, from two to ten at major research universities, are full-time at the university; they monitor administrative systems, operations, and procedures, as well as check expenditures for allowance under grants or contracts and audit indirect-cost rate proposals.

One might think that this third layer should be the last, and it usually is. But sometimes congressional committees will send auditors from the General Accounting Office (GAO) to audit the other government auditors. The more the HEW or DCAA auditors learn about how to nourish research and the more they work toward enhancing the research enterprise, the more suspicious their role becomes in the eyes of the GAO.

Who audits the GAO? It is wiser not to ask.

Under most conditions, the principal investigator does not feel the weight of this pyramid on his back. Although no one has ever calculated how much more research could be supported if this towering apparatus was made leaner, the investigator can frequently ignore it all.

There is a growing intrusion, however, into the control of the investigator's research. Much of this has originated in the circumstance that the work of a typical principal investigator is now usually supported by more than one agency—in pathological cases, sometimes by five or six agencies. As federal funds for research have decreased (in terms of constant dollars), and as the number of able (and hungry) investigators has increased, and as even basic research has become more "directed" by federal program managers, scientists have turned to more than one agency to support the work of their laboratories. Usually the agencies themselves encourage this; the agency is known by its "stable" of investigators, and it can continue to support (some of) the work of the well-known Dr. X at lower cost if other agencies share in the cost of his laboratory.

Separate proposals are written to the separate agencies, and sometimes there are even sharply delineable projects such that, say, the NSF could support a graduate student or post-doctoral fellow on a project totally separate from that of another individual supported by the NIH, both of whom are working for the same principal investigator. Usually, however, a *cordon sanitaire* cannot be drawn in the laboratory. Equipment, technicians, and space are shared, and ideas, which are the heart of the whole enterprise, recognize no boundaries. The principal investigator, while extremely conscientious to make sure federal funds are not wasted or mis-spent for personal profit, may under such circumstances become careless about the boundary between what NSF pays for and what NIH pays for. He *knows* that he is giving the project "his all," he *knows* that the research will eventually be of benefit to the people whom the government represents, and he never was very clear about the difference in interests (if any) between NSF and NIH.

The auditors' view is, of course, sharply different. The grant or contract papers with respect to which they are comparing the actual expenditures are written as if the NSF was buying n mops and the NIH was buying m brooms. Congress in its (finite?) wisdom specified the budgets of the two agencies. How, then, can a mere principal investigator arrogate to himself the right to raise one budget and lower the other? "Disallowed."

One can be wholly sympathetic with the role of auditors in preventing the *misuse* of federal funds, even if one can cavil at the number of auditors and the multiple layers.[1] But auditors produce only inefficiency, and put blinders on research when they attempt to restrict every dollar to the precise purpose they think Congress had in mind, when neither they nor the Congress understand the research. The overauditing is particularly reprehensible, since in no way can the university gain at federal expense by flexibility in the use of research funds; the university does not make a profit, and is "in business" solely for service, either to subsequent generations through teaching and research or to the present generation by direct public service.

Another arena of fiscal overregulation is the control of allowed "indirect costs"—frequently called "overhead," but more properly called "pooled costs." These are the costs of heat, light, maintenance, security, accounting, personnel offices, libraries, administration, and other general costs, which are just as "real" costs as the direct payroll costs on a particular project. Since it would cost too much to have an electric meter for every room or to bill each project separately for the costs of writing salary checks, these costs are pooled; each project then is charged a fairly determined fraction of the total. Most of the allocation is to teaching and other activities *not* paid for by federal funds, so the university and the investigators have a strong incentive to keep down the costs of maintenance, libraries, utilities, personnel and accounting services, and the like. The investigator and his supporting agency have an additional incentive to keep the allocation (through the "overhead rate") to his project down, since a fixed amount of grant money cannot produce as much research if a larger fraction is consumed by the electric bill (via the indirect cost allocation). Thus, the investigator and his agency are arrayed against the institution when indirect cost rates are under discussion. This polarization is damaging to morale and, ultimately, to research.

Recently this tension has been further exacerbated by the Office of Management and Budget (OMB). There is no new legislation, but OMB has decided to open up the longstanding treaty (known as "Budget Circular A-21") between the government and the universities which governs allocations of pooled costs. The motivations for this move seem to have been distrust, lack of standardization of accounting methods, and "to save the government money," although fear of powerful figures in Congress may also have played a role. Although there is inevitably some arbitrariness in assigning the costs of, say, the library to the various functions of a university (including research), there is no evidence that the government was paying more than its share. In OMB's suggested revisions, *every* change was in the direction to reduce the fraction applicable to sponsored research. Now the government can drive as hard a bargain as it wishes, but it and the country will not be well served by exploiting the universities (paying less than a fair share of pooled costs) even more than it did under the "old" A-21. The modest institutional grants have disappeared (except for a program in NIH); these grants used to provide some funds for universities to use for shared equipment, for facilities, for installation costs of government-furnished equipment, for risk-taking on research projects too inchoate to compete for federal funds, and in general for the "mortar between the blocks" of grants and contracts. Further erosion of the government's fair share of pooled costs represents a *negative* institutional support that damages the institutions and their ability to support faculty and facilities. Furthermore, no federal money will really be saved, since the universities have no profit and will simply have to cut out costs such as books, faculty salaries, and renovations. The proposed changes will simply drive the balance of costs of research more toward hourly salaries and expendable materials, and less toward professorial salaries, research equipment, and renewed facilities. Skewing this balance is not auspicious for the quality of research.

These problems arise because universities by their very nature deliver a *joint product*; teaching, public service, and research are all accomplished by the same faculties, laboratories, libraries, and computing centers. In a great university, advanced teaching and research are inextricably interwoven. Indeed, William G. Bowen has made the excellent point that the better the university functions, the more difficult it is to unscramble the costs—to assign a separate cost to each function. Attempts to make universities more fiscally responsible, in the narrow OMB sense, must therefore diminish their service in both teaching and research.

There are joint performers, as well as joint products, in research in universities. Recently the Internal Revenue Service (IRS) has attempted to redefine a graduate student as distinct from an employee (one need not ask in which direction the IRS was moving). A graduate student working on a sponsored research project is *both* a student and an employee. Like the question of a wave-particle in quantum mechanics, only those who do not have any understanding of the situation even attempt to draw a distinction. The reason it matters is, of course, that accommodation to whatever distinction the IRS ultimately invents will place arbitrary limitations on the way the student-employee learns and serves.

Research in the natural sciences inevitably leads investigators into unplanned paths and faces them with unexpected findings. The flexibility that is needed for effectiveness and efficiency in such an undertaking is anathema to government planners and auditors. They need, or think they need, sharp distinctions and definitions. But, as the discussion of the joint products and joint performers indicates, these distinctions are just not there. The conflict is reminiscent of one of the (largely irrelevant) arguments between "the theologian" and "the scientist," so popular in the last third of the nineteenth century. The one in question went something like this: The theologian said, "A scientist attempting to learn the ultimate structure of the universe is like a blind man looking in a dark cellar for a black cat that isn't there." The scientist replied, "Yes, you are perfectly right. But the theologian is also a blind man looking in a dark cellar for a black cat that isn't there; the difference is, he finds the cat." The government auditors will find the cat, even though it is not there.

What has happened to cause the transition from the government/university partnership of the early postwar period to the present uneasy and inefficient relation? Although the question cannot be answered with any completeness or confidence, some elements of the answer are doubtless the following:

(1) The experience of World War II has receded into history. Only a tiny fraction of policymakers have had any direct experience with how science worked for the country then.

(2) Science as the base for U.S. success in world markets is invisible. Congress and the administration do not understand the involved and convoluted connections between, say, support of helium liquefiers in 1950 and sale of computers or jet engines abroad in 1980.

(3) The country is not so frightened of the technological prowess of potential adversaries as it was at the time of the Korean war, the Soviet hydrogen bomb, or Sputnik.

(4) The country has been frightened by media speculation (there being no consequential U.S. incidents) about the dangers of some of the fruits of science, especially drugs and nuclear reactors.

(5) Scientists have oversold the practical benefits of science; perhaps the most prominent example is the prediction by high energy physicists in 1946 that vast new energy sources (comparable to the nuclear reactor) would flow if the government built big accelerators.

(6) The education that is inextricably tied to research no longer has the same political clout, since there are more than enough places for every potential student (except, probably for only a short time, in medicine and veterinary medicine).

(7) Congress has become occupied with the practice of confronting society's problems with direct action by overwhelming any problem with appropriated money; modest appropriations for developing understanding come later.

What of the future? It is unlikely that the efficient and productive partnership will return, at least in the next few years. The forces enumerated in the foregoing are still too powerful, even though the national need (especially in new sources of energy) for increased scope and effectiveness of research is stronger than ever. The universities, having lost hope of that return, would be happy if only a little more *stability* could be injected into federal support and regulation of research.

The universities built research facilities and expanded permanent faculties in response to the social goal of the 1950s and 1960s that more Ph.D.s should be educated to provide teachers and research workers, especially in the physical sciences, mathematics, and engineering. Washington was stimulating universities to expand in these decades by a multiplicity of fellowships and research support grants. For example, the President's Science Advisory Committee called in late 1962 for a *doubling* by 1970 in the number of doctor's degrees to be given in engineering, mathematics, and the physical sciences. Yet Bernard Berelson (1960:69–80) had already showed that supply and demand were likely to be in good balance *without* substantial increases in "production" rates. Furthermore, Allan Cartter (1966) was only a little later (fall 1965) in predicting a *surplus* of Ph.D.s. The federal momentum nevertheless persisted,[2] and only in the middle 1970s did the agencies begin talking of a "Ph.D. glut." The important point here for research is not to point the finger at slow or clumsy federal response to changing needs, but is to emphasize that federal stimulation grossly expanded the setting within which research is performed in the universities. Most universities now find themselves with faculties and plants in mathematics, physical sciences, and engineering that are too large to be nourished with high-quality research programs.

The cycle may be repeating in the biological sciences and medicine, until now still areas of growth. There are still federal capitation programs (federal subvention of so much per head of the number of medical students above some historical base) in medicine to encourage expansion, yet the Secretary of Health, Education, and Welfare (Califano 1978) has said that "we face in the next decade an over-supply of doctors."

There is national concern about the costs of health care, but national indecision whether these costs would be lowered by adding doctors (classical economics) or raised (a Parkinsonian theory that welfare and insurance agencies will pay for more patient visits and operations if there are more doctors). In the face of this confusion, universities and their medical schools cannot plan the size of their teaching and associated research facilities. The quality of research will suffer from this irregular federal regulation.

III

We turn now to more "conventional" regulation of research—that is, regulation more similar to that described in other chapters of this book. Because regulation is so varied and pervasive, it is possible to give only a small sampling, and only a snapshot of a rapidly moving process. The *Federal Register* has become required reading for research administrators, and the pages of *Science* each week reveal new regulations.

The magazine *Science* is, in fact, part of the problem. Congressional staffs and policymakers in OMB frequently think of *Science* as the house organ of science. After all, it is published by the American Association for the Advancement of Science and is supported by scientists' dues; one might be justified in thinking that it is biased toward scientists and science in the same way he expects the publication of an industrial corporation to put the corporate best foot forward. But some of the writers of the "News and Comment" section, far from being biased toward science, seem to enjoy an "academic freedom" to produce vivid writing in the style of the newsmagazines. If this controversy-generating reporting is read as if it is science speaking on its own behalf, it is small wonder that distrust of science and scientists pervades the Congress and the agencies.

Distrust, however caused, and political opportunism lead to control and regulation. The natural sciences are certainly not alone among activities in the United States in receiving this treatment. There may be, however, some special vulnerabilities of scientific research to conventional regulation:

(1) Congress is even less well prepared and well equipped to deal knowledgeably with hadron-hadron interactions, quadrupole source modeling of earthquakes, and organo-metallic free radicals than it is with the money supply.[3]

(2) Science is basically exploration, and *any* blinders or hobbles are particularly damaging when advancing into the unknown.

(3) Regulation of research must, in the end, be quantitative, and neither the Congress, the "public interest" groups, the courts, or the media are good at numbers (even *Science* reveals that its writers are over their heads by such abominations as "watts per day").[4]

(4) The public makes no distinction between science and applied science, and applied science has occasionally produced some rather frightening items. Nuclear weapons and thalidomide come first to mind. "It is easier to scare people than to unscare them"; a single headline about what "might" happen requires volumes of testimony to convince policymakers of what doubtless *will* happen. Scientists themselves are frequently responsible for the scaring, learn too late that they have overdone it, and learn the basic irreversibility summarized in this aphorism.

(5) Federal regulations respond to the winds of the interests of perceived constituencies. Science and basic research in particular are for the benefit of the twenty-first century, and there is no constituency for the twenty-first century.

(6) Universities and university research thrive on the academic freedom of the individual faculty investigator. With this goes decentralized management, in which the "principal investigator" (the sole faculty person on a grant, or one of

only two or three) controls the project and its use of federal funds. It is a damaging diversion for him to make himself an expert on all federal regulations, yet he can hardly relinquish control to a central administration.

The first examples of regulation we shall consider share the characteristic that they are intended to guarantee absolute *safety*, either of the scientists and their associates, or of the population generally. The preoccupation with safety is a recent phenomenon, but it has taken hold so universally and absolutely that this generation hardly recognizes the possibility of a different world. Certainly the eighteenth and even the nineteenth century frontier in the United States was a thoroughly unsafe place, not to mention the foolhardiness of Columbus and his followers of the sixteenth century. I get in over my philosophical depth very rapidly in pursuing the obvious question: was the quality of life worse on the frontier, with its shared risks and responsibilities, than in the present safety-conscious world, where many people's entire lives are spent (wasted?) in adding some tiny fraction of a percent to the almost hundred percent safety of living? Is there some human affinity for risk, excitement, and even danger that drives the worker, thoroughly protected from punch-press and steam-boiler accidents on the job, to drive home helmetless on a motorcycle or with seat belt unfastened in an automobile, or even intoxicated in either vehicle? Even to ask such questions makes one subject to accusations of callousness and lack of feeling. Yet science *is* a frontier, and there is no way of making the unknown safe.

But the federal regulators try. The Occupational Safety and Health Act (OSHA) of 1970 was aimed primarily at industrial accidents, but every activity, including the natural sciences, is caught up in it. Like most regulations, there are three levels of OSHA, and each has its problems.

First, there is the act itself. Its aim is a perfectly reasonable social goal—namely, that workers should not be subjected to unnecessary hazards on their jobs, jobs that increasingly relate workers to sophisticated machinery and expose them to a bewildering array of chemical species. One can still ask, however: How nearly absolute is this social goal if it comes in conflict with other equally or more appealing goals?

Second, there is the level of rule-making. Hundreds of pounds of regulations have been written, almost invariably with the worker in mind who is exposed to industrial quantities (not infrequently, carload lots) of chemicals, or is exposed for forty hours per week to noise or electrical hazards. The rule writers cannot possibly imagine *all* of the circumstances, especially in a scientific laboratory, but the rules make no provision for commonsense modifications suited to the laboratory scale of operations. Indeed, all of OSHA's millions of words applicable to medical research can be easily condensed to a simple statement: thou shalt not have medical research. This situation necessarily produces a "government of men, not of laws," since so much is prohibited that research can go on only by the wisdom of selective enforcement.

The third level is thus the enforcement. Up to the time of this writing, enforcement as it affects research has been largely carried out without serious damage. Educating the enforcement teams sometimes required many days, but in the end they exercised self-restraint and good judgment. (This differs sharply from the experience of enforcement of nondiscrimination regulations, discussed elsewhere in this book.) Research has not yet suffered except by the raising of costs common to all regulation, but it remains a hostage to the sweeping regulations.

There is an additional danger, especially in university research laboratories. Laboratory safety is a serious business, and an essential part of scientific education, especially of graduate students, is the training of each new generation in a careful, cautious, but commonsense approach to laboratory dangers. Physics laboratories will necessarily have "haywired" apparatus with lethal voltages; chemistry and biology laboratories will necessarily have powerful poisons and infectious agents. It would be tragic if students' contempt for the woodenness and inflexibility of OSHA regulations were to divert their attention from the absolutely necessary individual and flexible, but careful and cautious, recognition of laboratory hazards and from devising sensible approaches to coping with them.

There are added potential difficulties in the case of toxic substances (for example, cadmium has recently been the focus of attention) or chemical carcinogens (such as polychlorinated biphenyls) because of the multiplicity of federal agencies in the act. The Occupational Safety and Health Administration, the Environmental Protection Agency, and the National Institute of Occupational Safety and Health all have some authority and responsibility in this area. I know of no substantial damage yet to research. But the region of freedom between what is required and what is forbidden becomes smaller each year, and when more than one federal agency has authority, there is always the possibility that what is required by one agency will be prohibited by another.

A final example of safety-related regulation is the problem of recombinant DNA (deoxyribonucleic acid). By about 1975, forty years of research on DNA—the basic material that carries the genetic code and thus controls growth, development, and differentiation of living organisms—had put biochemists in an extremely powerful position. They could begin to do experiments in which DNA was segmented and reconstituted more or less by design, which creates the conceptual possibility of producing new species of living things.

These experiments were naturally widely reported, and occasioned a great deal of frightening speculation. Many scientists themselves, evidently anxious to avoid the accusation of irresponsibility, made rather flamboyant claims for the potentiality of recombinant DNA research, both for good and for evil (for example, a lethal virus that could replicate itself with no possibility of control once the "genie was outside the bottle"). This situation obviously invited regulation. Although municipal governments were concerned first, clearly the federal government would eventually be the controlling agent.

The first tries at federal legislation and regulation would have arrested recombinant DNA research and made the whole field chaotic. One proposal that almost survived, for example, would have permitted local governments to add additional controls to the federal regulations. The scientists themselves learned the truth of the aphorism cited earlier about "unscaring" the population as they worked hard to produce more moderate and sensible regulation. As a result of tremendous effort of this kind, the 1976 *NIH Guidelines* were modified to differentiate further among levels of risk. But the 1978 *Guidelines*, while explicitly acknowledging possible benefits from the research, still seem too restrictive to many workers in the field, and they certainly are overly detailed and bureaucratic. Scientists continue to work to modify the regulations, in keeping with the present conviction that the risks had been greatly exaggerated. It appears that after three or four years of hard work, the threat to shut down this whole field has been countered, albeit at an enormous cost in the diversion of scientists from science. There remains, too, the question of how sensible will be the federal monitoring of the research to verify compliance with the *Guidelines*.

Experimentation on human subjects is now subject to detailed regulation by HEW, including specification of the composition of the local committees to review research protocols. Virtually all major research institutions have for many years treated such research with great care; as public sensitivity and concern grew, review procedures were established at each institution so that the investigator, in his "total war" attitude toward his own research, would not invade the rights of others. There is little evidence, if any, that a federal regulatory overlay was needed. Indeed, the only well-publicized deficiencies of the voluntary system have been in the military services and in penitentiaries, operated by governments. Yet now there is considerable rigidity, and there are new requirements for documentation of consent that delay or prevent research and make it difficult to change directions in response to new ideas or new findings as the research progresses.

Much research on new drugs is prevented completely by restrictions on experimentation on human subjects in the United States. Our country has thus slipped into a curiously inconsistent position with other countries, especially less well-developed ones. We are noisily avoiding even the vestiges of colonialism, and yet we exploit other countries by insisting that our drugs be developed there, by, in effect, claiming that our population should not be subjected to the same risks as theirs.

Regulations for the care of laboratory animals are not yet so intrusive; despite powerful threats, no research is prevented and the directions of research are not constrained. But the regulations substantially raise the costs of research (and therefore diminish the quantity of research) and, like all other regulations, require massive documentation. Furthermore, it is not at all clear what public purpose is served by compulsory raising of the standard of living of laboratory animals vastly in excess of that of the American farm.

Classification—the prevention of publication by stamping "Secret" or "Confidential" on research results—was feared by all as the potentially most damaging of all regulation when the modern era of federal sponsorship of research began. It is refreshing to be able to report that classification has not turned out to be a major problem. There have been isolated areas where classification has been threatened or actually imposed—laser fusion, the gas centrifuge and laser isotope separators, and "unbreakable" encryption systems, for example. These events have been painful to the scientists involved, and wholly unnecessary. But they represent a tiny fraction of natural science research. Incidentally, publication of similar research by foreign scientists played a major role in all of these incidents in tempering overzealous classifiers.

It is difficult to state just why classification has *not* been more of a problem. Congress finds it hard to understand why it should support research that is freely published and available (at least in summary, written form) to all. It would simplify the task of the program manager who is defending his request for a congressional appropriation if he could point to classified outcomes. Perhaps the thwarting of the threat of classification is the result of a general recognition that military security and survival in world markets are attained by aggressive achievement, not by secrecy. Perhaps the lesson was learned from the transistor that open publication, and the rapid development of the field that accompanies it, provided the United States with more of an advantage over our competitors than secrecy would have provided. Whatever the reasons, the nearly complete absence of classification "hassles" has been highly beneficial for science. Publication in the open literature is vital to the health of science, since only by such dissemination can research results be studied, verified, extended, and built upon by all those with interest and ideas.

Federal regulation in the area of patents has been a more painful experience. Congress and the agencies have been so afraid of giving away something that was created at public expense that they have interfered with research, stifled government/university/industry cooperation, and denied the public the early fruits of exploitation of research. Part of the problem has been that inventions arising from research are not at all like the hula-hoop or the stepladder, inventions in which the basic idea is all important, and subsequent exploitation of the idea in production presents few problems. Virtually all patents arising from research require enormous subsequent investment to develop them and to make them available to the public. The inventor's conception is only the first step in a long process involving great risks. Therefore, flexible financial arrangements, providing in many cases for exclusive licenses for limited periods of time, are required if an idea is to become useful. Many government agencies and members of Congress have found exclusivity hard to swallow.

Another stumbling block in patent regulation was created by the Atomic Energy Commission when it forced a contractor to contribute his background patents in the field of the contract. The most experienced potential contractor had the most to lose, and the newcomer to the field—who often wished to become experienced at public expense—was favored. Research and development by the most capable performers was not the most likely outcome.

In the mid-1970s, many federal officials spoke out in favor of university/industry cooperative research. There was even some research support by the National Science Foundation and others that encouraged such relations. But the federal patent regulations are even more eloquent in discouraging this type of cooperation, and in rendering unlikely the early use by the public of any inventions that require major investment to exploit. Even those agencies that do not insist that the corporation bring its own background patents into the contract for use by the government insist that the government be given a royalty-free license for any patent that was conceived in a project, if even a tiny amount of federal support aided that project. In some cases, such as guidance for missiles, the government is the only potential customer. In others, such as nuclear waste disposal, no one knows what fraction of the business will be handled by the U.S. government. Industry, therefore, finds it hard to contribute its funds to joint projects when, even if the project was wildly successful technically and commercially, the eventual return to industry for its investment is problematic.

There is probably no absolutely fair patent regulation policy for government/industry/university cooperative projects, but there is a simple policy that should be much more fair than current policies and, at the same time, more likely to lead to early public use of inventions. That policy would be to assign any patents to one of the trio to administer, and to have all three share in the royalties in proportion to their shares of support. In principle, any one of the three could be the administrator. But the government has a miserable track record of rendering patents useful, and is not in a position to invest money, build pilot plants, and make other moves that would be required; contracting by the government with other companies could accomplish this, but if occasionally one such company profited substantially, there would be enormous pressure to become less flexible. The industrial partner has the most experience and financial capability, but may sometimes be constrained by antitrust considerations or may not be sufficiently interested in deviating from the heartland of its current products. The university would have to administer by contracting with companies, but still might be the best one of the three to hold the patents. Whichever partner was chosen, there should be complete freedom to grant licenses on whatever terms would lead to most productive exploitation. The people's interests would thereby be served best not only through early use, but also by reimbursement of the federal government for part of the costs of the research—or even for *more* than the costs of the research upon occasion.

IV

This has been a gloomy story. Of course, each of us believes his own problems are the most refractory, but I have tried to show that there really are some especially damaging effects of federal regulation upon the natural sciences.

The situation may even be on the verge of further deterioration. Research survives because of the wisdom, experience, and dedication of many agency heads and program managers in Washington. A generous sprinkling of "short-timers"—scientists, engineers, and physicians whose major careers have been at the laboratory bench—has been extremely helpful in rationalizing the regulatory process.

Sanity in the regulation of research, and the federal administration of research programs, probably received a setback with the 1978 Ethics in Government Act.[5] Among other prohibitions, the act prohibits any government employee of, say, HEW from having, for at least a year after leaving HEW, the kind of contact with HEW all researchers in biology and medicine must have. It promises to be extremely difficult under the new law to attract into government posts anyone with research experience, since his options after leaving the government will be severely limited. Without the tempering effect of policymakers who have tried to pry nature's secrets from her, and who know the frustrations and damaging diversions associated with that complicated process, one can expect that regulation of research will become even more wooden.

Gloomy as the story is, science continues. Fortunately, its vitality is continually enhanced by new generations of bright young people, hard working under adverse conditions and not easily discouraged. For the real scientist, curiosity, the inability to rest when there is something still to be learned about the natural world, is a powerful driving force that surmounts almost all obstacles. Yet one wonders why the United States is willing to permit clumsy regulation to threaten its precious advantage of world leadership in natural science.

5

MIRO M. TODOROVICH

A Road to Stalemate—the Current State of Regulations

The Supreme Court and employment practices. The search for affirmative action violations. Equal protection and reverse discrimination. EEOC regulations. The *Uniform Guidelines on Employee Selection Procedures*. Educational nightmares from federal interference. Weaknesses in the system of checks and balances.

Equal opportunity planners and their supporters have, over the years, proceeded along two avenues of argument—one based on the 1971 *Griggs v. Duke Power* decision of the

Supreme Court, and the other based on President Johnson's Executive Order 11246 against discrimination, issued on 24 September 1965 and amended in 1967 to include sex along with race, color, religion, and national origin.

The *Griggs* decision held that employment practices which are "neutral on their face and even neutral in term of intent" violate the Civil Rights Act if they "'freeze' the status quo of prior discriminatory employment practices." The *Griggs* decision proscribes both overt discrimination and practices that are "fair in form, but discriminatory in operation." Thus, the Supreme Court declared that it is not necessary to prove intent to establish discrimination. Even if employment tests are created with no desire to discriminate, once they disproportionately affect blacks and other protected groups they must be abolished and remedies instituted. These considerations had far-reaching consequences for the institutions of higher learning.

The *Griggs* dictum yielded four main action items:

(1) Since the employer's intent is secondary in importance, government contractors, including colleges and universities, must analyze the *results* of their current employment practices—even if they believe that they have never discriminated and have never been charged with discrimination.

(2) Any employment practice which produces a disproportional impact of hirees from protected racial and other backgrounds is discriminatory and should be changed.

(3) Numerical mismatches between employers' "work force" and available applicant pool is proof of discrimination and should trigger a remedy.

(4) Employers should implement voluntary remedies to correct past wrongs, without waiting for legal actions to compel remedies.

The first of these points is most important, since it triggers the other three. Indeed, activist proponents always maintained that without internal self-surveys, monitored by government agencies, an employer cannot even know whether his actions have led to discriminatory results.

Critics responded that when the crime is defined only *after* the investigation is over, the rules mandating employer self-analysis can be stacked to make the guilty verdict a foregone conclusion. This actually seems to have happened everywhere the Office for Civil Rights (OCR) of the Department of Health, Education, and Welfare (HEW) has undertaken exemplary comprehensive reviews. Yearlong investigations became legalized "fishing expeditions" in which regional OCR investigators prowled through accumulated data in search of "damning" numerical discrepancies.[1] As soon as such statistical mismatches were revealed—and they were inevitable because of the limited available pool of qualified minority applicants—remedies would automatically be triggered. As Robert G. Dixon, Jr., has written in a paper presented to a plenary session on *Bakke,* Association of American Law Schools (annual meeting at Chicago, 4 January 1979):

> The civil rights agencies and the lower federal courts developed a simple litigation proof formula. That formula unabashedly uses gross population figures. Racial nonproportionality is easily shown. A judicial order commanding some form of racially preferential hiring or admission procedure follows as a matter of course, because the defendant is almost in the impossible situation of proving a negative.

In practice, Presidential Order 11246 complemented *Griggs* very well. The latter supplied the principles, while the former provided a vehicle for activism. The order charged the Department of Labor with writing rules for implementation. To a lay reader, the order seems eminently clear and simple:

> The contractor will not discriminate against any employee or applicant for employment because of race, color, religion, sex, or national origin. The contractor will take affirmative action to ensure that applicants are employed, and that employees are treated during employment, without regard to their race, color, religion, sex, or national origin.

The Labor Department rulewriters insisted, however, that the practical actions must be "result oriented," and demanded that every contractor above a certain size use self-analysis as a basis for an affirmative action (AA) plan. In elaborating Order 11246, Order No. 4 introduced concepts like "underutilization," "available or traditional hiring pool," "affected class," "goals and precise timetables," and "preferred or protected groups," none of which appears in the presidential order. The required self-analysis could not by itself *prove* that discriminatory practices ever existed, nor was it intended to. But it became immensely coercive, as indicated by its incorporation into the equal employment concept:

> An affirmative action program is a set of specific and result-oriented procedures to which a contractor commits himself to apply every good faith effort. *The objective of those procedures plus such efforts is equal employment opportunity.* . . . An acceptable affirmative action program must include an analysis of areas within which the contractor is deficient in the utilization of minority groups and women, and further, goals and timetables to which the contractor's good faith efforts must be directed to correct the deficiencies and, thus to increase materially the utilization of minorities and women, at all levels and in all segments of his work force where deficiencies exist. [Emphasis added]

According to Order No. 4, the AA plans are *sine qua non* for government contracts. And if, over a thirty-day "show cause" period, the contractor is not brought into compliance, the compliance agency, with approval of the director, "shall promptly commence formal proceedings leading to the cancellation or termination of existing contracts or subcontracts and debarment from future contracts and subcontracts."

These arm-twisting provisions convert the past hiring practices in colleges and universities into extremely race-conscious and gender-conscious procedures with racial surveys, quotas, and all that the presidential order seems to have proscribed. Thus, Order No. 4 became the implementational arm of *Griggs*. It forced otherwise innocent parties to engage in reverse discrimination in order to remedy alleged past injustices by fixing up set numerical ratios, and thus to avoid the loss of critically needed government funding, including loans to students.

These affirmative action drives were both severe and rampant in the early 1970s, but for several reasons they began to diminish in the latter part of the decade. First, it became apparent that fewer qualified applicants were available to adjust the numbers than the agencies had anticipated. Second, the high cost of the AA programs also affected their rate of implementation. And finally, HEW, which the Labor Department delegated to administer the program for colleges and universities, became overwhelmed by the very paperwork it helped to generate. The affirmative action plans, surveys, and the like were coming in faster than the Office for Civil Rights could digest.

Recently a new twist has developed. Inside and outside the academy, individuals victimized by reverse discrimination have sought redress in the courts under the equal protection clause. The well-known *Bakke* Supreme Court decision, though not involving employment and government regulations, did raise questions of the fairness of affirmative action, and it has had a chilling effect on some of its more ardent and ruthless practitioners.

A more important regulation case, this one involving reverse discrimination in employment, is *Weber v. Kaiser Aluminum,* which the Supreme Court accepted in December 1978. In *Weber,* the lower courts have ruled that Kaiser has committed reverse discrimination; they found no prior discrimination to be remedied, and they also found that the advancement quota did not benefit any identifiable victim of past discrimination. In finding that Kaiser's goal was a quota, they ruled that the company's and the union's action violated Title VII of the Civil Rights Act of 1964. The lower courts also declared provisions of OFCC (Office of Federal Contract Compliance) Order No. 4 to be in violation of Title VII to the extent that they induced, by governmental coercion, the defendant's actions. If the Supreme Court upholds the lower court rulings, the result will be reinterpretation of all regulations in this area. One result will be that affirmative action plans in universities and elsewhere will have to become truly nondiscriminatory in intent and evenhanded and fair in execution.

A renewed study of *Griggs* provided affirmative action critics with some fresh ammunition. They argued that in opposing "unnecessary barriers to employment" the justices did not intend to void genuine qualifications needed for performance of a job. The court held that the key issue is "business necessity."

> Congress has not commanded that the less qualified be preferred over the better qualified simply because of minority origins. Far from disparaging job qualifications as such, Congress has made such qualifications the controlling factor so that race, religion, nationality and sex become irrelevant.

To critics, this meant—and lower courts began to agree—that job-related tests, required by business necessity, may be legitimate, even though they have a disproportionate impact on women or minorities. Indeed, the justices in *Griggs* stated quite explicitly that the 1964 Civil Rights Act "does not command that any person be hired simply because he was formerly the subject of discrimination or because he is a member of a minority group. Discriminatory preference for any group, minority and majority, is precisely and only what Congress has proscribed."

Thus, affirmative action theory comes back full circle. The theory began with a demand for remedies, even without prior discriminatory intent or proof of wrongdoing. Mere numerical mismatch triggered reparations—supervised by an elaborate bureaucratic mechanism. At that point, the result-oriented outcome meant quotas, explicitly or implicitly, with proportional distribution of jobs among contesting groups of citizens. If the result was discrimination against "others," it was dismissed as justified retribution for the sins of earlier generations. Gradually, however, the underlying theoretical momentum was eroded by a more careful reading of *Griggs*, by the stand of most courts against blanket quotas, by the removal in *Bakke* of race as a unilateral parameter, and by the courts' refusal to mandate remedies without a prior finding of wrongdoing or of identifiable victims.

In short, the courts now seem to be holding that equal protection still applies to every individual, that both corporate entities and individuals are innocent until proven guilty, and that rewards for past suffering or for a job well done should go to relevant persons, not to accidental members of some favored groups.

THE NEW REGULATORY STRATEGY

To vitiate the emerging stalemate and put the federal regulatory drives back on course, bureaucratic strategists in recent months have developed two new approaches, both rooted in *Griggs*. One would revive pressures under Order No. 4 and similar ordinances. The other would make it difficult and costly for employers to prove the job-relatedness of tests or other hiring procedures which disproportionately impact governmentally favored groups.

The Equal Employment Opportunity Commission (EEOC), having enforcement responsibility, had already issued guidelines interpreting parts of the 1964 Civil Rights Act when *Griggs* reached the Supreme Court in December 1970. In its decision, the court stated that "great deference" should be given to such guidelines. Eight years later EEOC decided to use that deference to abort potential reverse discrimination cases.[2] In December 1977 it developed a series of regulations legalizing reverse discrimination if an employer has a "reasonable basis" for believing that he might be in violation of Title VII and adopts an affirmative action plan to remedy the problem.[3] Moreover, the exemption holds even without a showing that Title VII has in fact been violated.

EEOC divides citizens into two groups: (1) those whom an employer (and EEOC rulemakers) would consider, upon "self-analysis," to be underrepresented in employment, and (2) "others." An employer is assured he can deny employment opportunity to "others" with complete impunity, even without evidence of prior discrimination. The mere belief of an employer that he might be violating Title VII permits him to discriminate. A second regulation explicitly permits "the use of race, color, sex, and ethnic-conscious goals and timetables, ratios, or other numerical remedies" in affirmative action programs to remedy prior discrimination.[4]

By emphasizing the remedial aspect of affirmative action programs, the proposed text made obvious EEOC's current commitment to racial and sexual quotas. At the same time, there were no proposed quotas based on national origin or religious preference. On this latter point, the proposed text advanced a selective interpretation of the complete statute, which actually commanded nondiscrimination on *all* grounds—not only on those of race and sex.

In Item 4, the EEOC created a tailor-made guideline to suit the discriminatory intent of its interpretation, and produced a perennial shield of immunity for employers who discriminate.[5] The message to the employers is quite clear: make a statistical self-analysis, deny employment to nonpreferred, claim that you are doing it according to EEOC guidelines and interpretation, and don't fear any consequences. According to the guidelines, cases brought to the commission by aggrieved persons will be dismissed without regard to the fact that the complainant has been denied employment because of ethnic origin or sex.

Finally, Item 5 stipulated:

> The specification of remedial and affirmative action in these Guidelines is intended only to identify certain types of actions which an employer or other person may take consistent with Title VII to comply voluntarily but does not attempt to provide standards for determining whether such attempts to eliminate discrimination against minorities and women have been successful. Whether, in

any given case, the employer who takes such remedial and affirmative action will have done enough to remedy discrimination against minorities and women under Title VII will be a question of fact in each case.

This section of the proposed guidelines contained two messages. One said that what is good enough to cause a complaint charging discrimination to be dismissed, and a discriminatory action to be sanctioned, is still not sufficient to indicate an employer's good-faith compliance efforts. The second message emphasized that the sufficiency of affirmative action efforts will be determined from the inquiry into the facts of each case. Curiously enough, nonpreferred applicants, as stated earlier, can be discriminated against without a finding or evidence that affirmative action was even necessary. As in many other bureaucratic regulations, the uses of such blatant double standards are justified by the pressing needs for result-oriented pragmatic action. Little thought is given to principles violated by such actions, or to the obligation that critical and far-reaching decisions be consistent with the clearly stated views of the legislative branch—Section 703 (j) of Title VII.

These proposed regulations caused a storm of protests from various civil rights and nondiscrimination groups. The critics noted that apart from being contradictory on their face, the rules create two classes of citizens—those who are preferred and those who can be discriminated against with impunity. This violates Order 11246, Section 703 (j), of the Civil Rights Act, as well as the constitutionally protected right of all citizens to equal protection under the law. Also, while the Civil Rights statute and the presidential order consider on equal footing discrimination because of race, sex, creed, and national origin, the guidelines single out sex and race for special treatment.

Moreover, the proposed text introduced the concept of "benefits" resulting supposedly from remedial—i.e., affirmative—action by an employer. *Nowhere* in the Civil Rights Act or the presidential order does one find reparational "benefits" which would result from application of the statutes. The statutes meant to assure nondiscriminatory treatment and to require affirmative action, including possible allocation of back pay with medical and fringe benefits, to ensure such equal opportunity and nondiscriminatory treatment for all those who may have, in the past, been *actual* victims of such discrimination. The aim of the statutes is clearly to secure equal opportunity for all—not to dispense unearned benefits to some.

The proposed text, quoted above, also created a strange mechanism for allocating supposed "benefits" by the employer or others to persons who are not identifiable victims of past discrimination. Such allocation could only be accomplished, as EEOC apparently wants to do, by establishing preferential groups; people lucky enough to be born into those groups would then possess special legal rights, including the right to benefits. Critics charged that this violates our constitutional commitment to equality under the law and equality of opportunity for individuals—as well as the constitution's abhorrence, more fundamentally, of any special treatment or favoritism for special groups or classes of citizens. Even a proposal for an *equal* treatment of groups, as distinct or opposed to equal treatment of individuals, would raise serious and difficult questions. Advocating *inequality* of groups—as done in the proposed guidelines—and offering some groups benefits not offered to others, seemed unconscionable.

Finally, opponents of EEOC's proposed guidelines viewed them as an invitation and virtual license for employers to discriminate. And this view was reinforced by earlier EEOC assurances that

> the lawfulness of such programs [i.e., of the denial of employment opportunity to some applicants] is not dependent upon an admission, or a finding, or evidence sufficient to prove that an employer . . . taking such action [denial of employment] has violated Title VII.

The guidelines extended the invitation also vis-à-vis any other federal or local statute, thus converting its nondiscriminatory intent into a discriminatory license.

Nevertheless, the EEOC brushed aside the criticism and issued final guidelines on 19 February 1979, albeit in somewhat toned-down and less explicit form. The main provisions of the draft remained intact.

The forementioned *Weber* case has a certain ironic interconnection with the workings of EEOC. Before going to court, Weber had approached the commission for help; but he got no action, ostensibly because it was overloaded with cases. Now that the agency is trying actively to prevent people like him from going to court, the *Weber* ruling, if upheld by the Supreme Court, may prove fatal to the commission's guidelines. In any case, there is already question whether the new rules are valid in the wake of *Bakke*. The Powell decision seems to go counter to most, if not all, main tenets of the EEOC ordinance.

The second new regulatory approach is contained in the *Uniform Guidelines on Employee Selection Procedures* (43 FR, pp. 38290–309, 25 August 1978), issued jointly by the EEOC, the Civil Service Commission, the Department of Justice, and the Department of Labor. These guidelines depart from the activist views of the mid-1960s, when tests were viewed as a subterfuge to perpetuate discrimination. At the time, civil rights groups pushed for the abolishment of all tests, and in *Griggs* the Supreme Court seemed to agree, except when they were job related. Now, ten years later, the four federal agencies are asking for the exact opposite, i.e., that *all* hiring be validated by tests adjusted to yield the required numerical percentages. The agencies apparently decided that qualifications are here to stay, and proceeded to design validation procedures for certifying qualifications which, in one way or another, will lead to the government quotas.

It is not easy to summarize—or even to disentangle—the many provisions found in the twenty pages of fine regulatory print. Nevertheless, certain points in the text of the *Uniform Guidelines* are unambiguous, and they reveal the essential features of the regulations, particularly as they apply to institutions of higher learning:

1. There is a clear new definition of discrimination: "Procedure having adverse impact constitutes discrimination unless justified." This puts the entire burden of proof on the shoulder of the "defendant." (In *Griggs* the burden of proof was on the *employer* who wished to use *a test*—a subtle but important distinction.) In a certain sense, the above quote constitutes a verdict prior to trial.

2. Often an employer will have to look for alternative selection procedures:

> [W]henever a validity study is called for . . . the user should . . . [investigate] alternative selection procedures . . . which will have as little adverse impact as possible. . . . Whenever the user is shown an alternative selection procedure with evidence of less adverse impact and substantial evidence of validity for the same job in similar circumstances, the user should investigate it to determine the appropriateness of using or validating it in accord with these guidelines.

In other words, the basic goal of a faculty selection process should not be the *best* available faculty, but one with "less adverse impact."

3. Information on impact will be gathered through recordkeeping covering "applicable race, sex, and ethnic groups" listed as follows:

> Blacks (negroes), American Indians (including Alaskan Natives), Asians (including Pacific Islanders), Hispanics (including persons of Mexican, Puerto Rican, Cuban, Central or South American, or other Spanish origin or culture regardless of race), whites (Caucasians) other than Hispanics.

This means that an "adverse impact" on Hispanics or American Indians will be observable, but not that on Polish Americans or citizens whose ancestors are from India.

4. The selection procedures for higher-level jobs are severely restrictive, which will be a problem in faculty hiring. Traditionally, a professor was not hired only to teach, for example, Economics I; he was hired because presumably he was a reputable scholar or had the potential to become one. He was hired for a "higher-level job." But under the new guidelines:

> [W]here job progression is not so nearly automatic, or the time span is such that higher level jobs or employees' potential may be expected to change in significant ways, it should be considered that applicants are being evaluated for a job at or near the entry level.

Although a "reasonable period of time" will vary for different jobs, it will seldom exceed five years. And procedures for higher-level jobs will not be allowed (a) if a majority of employees "do not progress to the higher level," (b) if doubt exists that the higher-level job "will continue to require essentially similar skills during the progression period," or (c) if qualities required for advancement are expected to develop primarily from experience on the job.

5. The rulemaker did allow for the possibility that fields may exist in which validity studies cannot be performed; but the suggested alternative procedure is not much simpler than the validation process. In capsule form, deans, department chairmen, search committees, and others are told: if you do not have scored procedures, invent some; if you used scored procedures, validate them; in any case, remove the "adverse impact" or you will have to "justify" your present practice. Such justification will be neither simple nor cheap.

6. Under present rules, justifying faculty and research hiring procedures as currently practiced will be time consuming and costly, and will involve comprehensive analyses, "measures

of dispersion," "biserial correlations," and extensive data reporting. There is one way an employer can avoid all the costs and bother associated with the validation process—the so-called "bottom line" concept. When the *overall* selection process does not have an adverse impact, the government will usually consider the process valid and not examine it. It is interesting that, during the comment period, employer groups argued that the bottom line should prohibit enforcement by federal agencies for any part of a selection process without adverse impact. But civil rights and some labor representatives expressed concern that the concept could be interpreted as a matter of law, and might allow certain discriminatory conditions to go unremedied.

The rulemakers revised the guidelines to clarify that the bottom line may be based upon administrative and prosecutorial discretion. Thus, if the agencies decide that quotas have been fulfilled and the bottom line is in order, the lucky—and perhaps clever—employer will save himself a lot of paperwork, cost, and bureaucratic bother.[6]

It will be some time before meaningful assessment of the new federal hiring regulations becomes possible. In untold ways, almost every column of fine print in the *Federal Register* may affect the structure, mission, and performance of educational and research institutions of the United States. If the application progresses in a piecemeal fashion, as was the case with Order No. 4, resistance to new regulations will remain scattered and ineffective, and colleges and universities may experience serious dislocations of their performance as well as of their mission. However, if the leadership of the various professional, educational, and scholarly organizations take a timely closer look at these employment procedures and develop a joint stand, this could blunt some of the potentially more damaging consequences of a literal and unrestricted application of the federal rules. It is clearly up to the professors to defend their ivory tower.

WHAT MADE OVERREGULATION POSSIBLE

The regulatory activities described earlier were but a wedge breaking the wall which previously shielded the intellectual and economic life from the whims of the government. There was a time when a desirable society consisted of an association of autonomous commercial, educational, and industrial units, each working under the least possible constraints for the general good of the country. Now the various levels of the mushrooming federal and local bureaucratic apparatus are spreading regulatory controls over almost everything—from the shape of the common ladder to the intricacies of genetic research.

In institutions of higher learning, for example, the government tries to dictate the restructuring of instruction, irrespective of costs, to suit blind and other handicapped students. In turn, authorities demand that alcoholics and addicts be kept in classrooms—whether as students or teachers—because HEW has classified them as handicapped. The same agency has also prohibited the posting of student grades, even by social security or any other numerical coding, without the written consent of the student for every separate course; according to this interpretation of the privacy statutes, the posting of scores in any athletic competition would require the *written* consent of every participant. Not so long ago, HEW tried also to outlaw father-and-son breakfasts in elementary and secondary schools. A public uproar gave the then President Ford sufficient leverage to quash such bureaucratic insensitivity.

Another set of educational nightmares emerged from the travails of the Commission for the Protection of Human Subjects. Initially perceived as guardian against possible abuse of physical experimentation with humans, the commission became an instrument for the development of wholesale impediments to *any kind* of academic and journalistic research involving human beings. Most certainly, one cannot accept the premise that the establishment of a historical record should hinge on the "informed consent" of the participants, as is required in physical experimentation. Equally unacceptable seem regulations which would, *as a matter of routine,* put the HEW or any other bureaucrat between the academic researcher and his object of research. Many social scientists and advocates of academic and intellectual freedom consider such regulatory developments, spearheaded by HEW, a grave attack on the very foundations of the liberal arts and social sciences, and have said so in their comments on the proposed regulations.

In certain areas, notably in the field of genetic engineering, vigorous protests from the ranks of the academic and research professionals have succeeded in preventing the development and implementation of some of the most sweeping and restrictive regulatory language. This offers some hope that resolute protests on the part of concerned professionals, acting as trustees of our intellectual and academic heritage, may erect some barriers to a runaway bureaucratic rulemaking. Academics, however, may be considered as warriors of last resort, taking arms only when the very survival of their specialty is at stake. Thus, one should probably expect more trying years ahead for the cause of academic and educational freedom.

In summary, one may observe that during the last ten years the institutions of higher learning and the country have been subjected to a veritable flood of regulations. Starting from somewhat vague—yet otherwise innocuous—legislation, various governmental agencies, as if in a race to outdo each other, have produced a web of ordinances which push the country towards a planned economy and severely regulate the life of our citizens. Examples of this trend are not difficult to find. The interpretation of the Toxic Substances Act as requiring a complete inventory of the production, sales, and use of *all* chemical substances will bring this industry under a centralized, "rational" supervision by governmental authorities.

In many states, utilities are becoming encrusted with governmental planning. Other deletereous consequences of proliferating regulations, like those encountered by the builders of the West Coast oil pipeline, are well known. On the level of the individual citizen, he or she will continue to face mounting restrictions in all aspects of personal life—from the choice of food and type of medication to the mode of travel, and from the choice of fabric for upholstery and children's wear to the type of housing and kinds of recreation.

It is of considerable interest to analyze the changed governmental climate which made such intrusions into the life of the nation possible.

Not so long ago, various levels of the federal and local governments were paying for the programs they were willing to implement or provide. Whether it was the Corps of Engineers or school lunch program, governmental decision-making involved budgets which had to be funded. If moneys were available, they were appropriated; institutions would exist and programs would run. If not, things would fold and disappear. The limited availability of funds was thus a natural check to the proliferation of unbalanced governmental activism.

One of the early breaches of the principle that the government should pay for its expectations was the shift of the burden of a large part of the cost of tax collection from the shoulders of the Internal Revenue Service and other tax-collecting agencies to the taxpayers themselves. Indeed, it became possible for the tax forms and reporting requirements to become as elaborate as the rulewriters could desire, without causing any substantial cost to the government. Still, the tax-collection task remained a narrow one, and consequently the associated free-riding regulatory expansions remained within tolerable bounds.

Things started to change more dramatically during the late 1960s. Governmental bureaucrats discovered that in the name of any of the good-sounding goals—nondiscrimination, occupational safety, healthy nutrition, nuclear safety, environmental protection, and many others—rulemakers could design orders, rules, guidelines, and the like which will not cost the government a penny. Bureaucracies thus find themselves free of traditional constraints. Imagination is now the only limit to runaway rulewriting, and the increased thickness of the *Federal Register* is an eloquent testimonial to its fruitfulness.

Another breach in tradition occurred in the area of those unlegislated rules which seem of unclear origin, but whose impact is easily recognized. Until recently, Congress or other legislative bodies voted into law bills of general purpose which required specific rules of implementation. Administrators were charged with formulating regulations covering the application of such statutes—regulations supposed to be within the boundaries of the original law.

Recent bureaucratic practices, buttressed by certain court decisions, used such laws as opportunities for rulemaking which far exceeded congressional intent. This rulemaking disregards the letter and spirit of the enabling legislation.

As a result of this regulatory boldness and the pass-along of costs to the governed, the country finds itself swamped by regulations which are deplored by many, but effectively countered by precious few. True, we are reaching a point of oversaturation, where the sheer cost of paperwork and the inability of agencies to handle their own volume of work puts a certain damper on the further expansion of rules. Still, there is little reason for comfort in a stalemate caused by stacks of unprocessed documents and pages of ill-conceived—and thus unenforceable—ordinances. Foolish rules breed disrespect and disobedience, and more of the same will not improve matters. What is needed is a creative analysis of the current regulatory tumor. We may discover that the checks and balances established many years ago by the Founding Fathers are just not enough to restrain the modern breed of coercive bureaucrats. Budget balancing by itself will probably not do. Viable democracy cannot be perpetuated by fiscal alacrity alone.

6

NATHAN GLAZER

Regulating Business and Regulating the Universities: One Problem or Two?

Early causes of government regulation. The changing attitudes of regulator and regulated. Abuses of regulation, blanketing, hostility. Application of industrial regulation to the campus. The functions of higher education as seen in Washington. Faculty reaction as regulator and as teacher/researcher. The "new" iron triangle.

The history of government regulation of business is much longer than that of government regulation of the universities and colleges.* Its purposes, until the middle 1960s or so, were also very different from the purposes of government regulation of the universities and colleges. Government regulation of business was punitive in its origins; of colleges and universities, benign. And, until recently, the attitude of business—and of universities and colleges—toward government and its expansion have also shown marked differences; business is suspicious, universities and colleges (at any rate, their faculties) are approving. Today, while many spokesmen of higher education (fewer spokesmen of business) try still to argue that the relations between government and higher education are simply going through some early growing pains and transitional difficulties, and that all in the end will be well, universities and colleges are increasingly finding that they, too, seem to have climbed into bed with an 800-pound gorilla rather than a benign teddy bear. It is an interesting story, for the curmudgeonly fears of politicians opposed in principle to government action—such as Barry Goldwater and John G. Tower—it turned out, are echoed fifteen years later by the presidents of Harvard and Yale, and by others who are very far from the views of Senators Goldwater and Tower.[1] How did it all happen? And is the convergence between the cries of alarm of business and higher education more apparent than real?

Certainly government regulation of business, in its inception, had very different causes from government regulation of higher education. Government regulation of business begins in a clearly adversary mode. Business has been guilty of actions against the national interest, and it would be regulated

*This article deals only with federal regulation of universities and business, and "government" should be taken to mean "federal government." States have a rather wider role in regulating universities than does the federal government, but it is the expansion of the federal role in regulation that has created the present mood of concern.

to prevent them. The railroads would not be allowed to raise rates unconscionably, to give rebates to favored customers, and the like. Big business would not be allowed to combine in restraint of trade. The producers of food and drugs would have to hold to a given standard so that they cannot poison their customers. Natural monopolies, or efficient monopolies—utilities, telephones—would be controlled in the public interest. The airlines would be controlled in the public interest, so that they would provide efficient and reliable service at a reasonable cost. Business would not be allowed to use unfair practices in preventing the organization into trade unions of its workers, and would have to bargain collectively with them. Business would not be allowed to exploit the public with deceptive securities. And so we had the ICC, the antitrust act, the Pure Food and Drug Act, the FTC, the FCC, the CAB, the SEC, the NLRB, and so on. Admittedly, some of this regulation does not have a purely antagonistic origin, but exists to foster and protect some branch of industry. More significantly, according to the analyses of political scientists, even if this nurturant attitude was not part of the origins of business regulation, in time the close relations between regulated and regulator led to the "capture" of the regulatory agencies, so that much of their activity was designed to protect the industry they were regulating.[2]

Nor has the newer social regulation been very different in its inception. The EEOC, OSHA, the EPA, and CPSC, are not considered particularly friendly to business, and were established to control what were seen primarily as business abuses. On the other hand, hardly anyone is claiming business has gotten very far in capturing *these* agencies.[3]

The contrast with the regulation of higher education could not be sharper. The regulation of American higher education by the federal government arises from what we would all consider entirely benign activities. Federal involvement with higher education had nothing to do at the beginning with any sense on anyone's part that there were abuses to be controlled. Rather, higher education was seen as a good thing. It was valuable for personal advancement, and thus access to higher education was a suitable reward to veterans—hence the GI Bill and the payment of World War II veterans' tuition. Institutions of higher education could advance American research capability and achievement—and so a second major involvement was the funding of research on American campuses. And it continued from there. Higher education was encouraged to provide the graduate scientists and specialists that the country needed to counter Russia's scientific achievement. It was used to maintain American preeminence in nuclear physics and in space research. It was to be supported with libraries and dormitories so as to permit it to expand and provide its benefits to more students. It was to be encouraged with grants to provide more doctors, dentists, and nurses, city planners and school administrators, and whatever other specialized professionals seemed to be in short supply. It was to be assisted by assisting students on various grounds to get higher educations—and thus dependents of social security recipients, poor students in general, and in time almost all students, were added to veterans as those deserving of aid of some type in getting a higher education.

Having presented the contrast between business, seen as rapacious in its profit-seeking and requiring severe regulation, and higher education, seen as benign and aided to assist national objectives, how did it happen that they both ended up in the same boat? One may ask further, does higher education possess certain characteristics important for our culture and society which make it singularly inappropriate for much of the regulation to which it is now subjected? Does the fastening of the same standards on business and education indicate some massive error which, properly pointed out, can be corrected, to the health of higher education and the society of which it is a part? These are some of the questions that this chapter addresses.

First, let us review how it happened that higher education came to be viewed by government regulators with something similar to the distance, suspicion, and hostility that were common in the regulation of business. There were three major routes to this final result.

The first was that real abuses developed as government contracted with higher education for services. The second was that the explosion of social regulation did not—perhaps could not—make distinctions as between profit-making and non–profit-making sectors of society; that it blanketed—more than earlier economic regulation specifically devoted to the abuses of a given industry or given practices had done—higher education into those who were to be regulated, along with all other employers or all other contractors with government. The third was that in time a real suspicion of higher educational institutions as such, and hostility toward them, developed among some important opinion-making sectors; they were seen as discriminatory, insensitive to new social demands, and elitist. Thus regulation, from dealing with *some* specific abuses in higher education, from unconsciously including higher education along with other enterprises to be regulated, moved to an adversary stance. Higher education, just as business, in the regulators' practice and orientation, was presumed guilty until proven otherwise.

Above these three specific routes to an adversary stance was the simple operation of bureaucracy and regulation. They expand. The reasons for regulation's expansion—beyond what is originally intended in legislation and in executive decree—are numerous. Regulation expands because it must be orderly; the original fault, whatever it may be, that occasioned intervention must lead to a general rule—which may lead to general supervision—whether one has committed the fault or not. Regulation expands because powerful interest groups put regulators under pressure. It expands, too, because the new availability of judicial forums in which to press demands for greater government regulation puts regulators under the pressure of courts. Regulation expands because Congress finds it easier to attack a specific problem in general than to prevent or correct the damage that occurs as its legislation is turned into rules—and is expanded in scope—by regulators. To attack a fault (discrimination against minorities, women, the handicapped, environmental degradation, abuse of human subjects) is a noble thing. To then go through the hard work of trying to contain the unintended consequences of eliminating the fault is a difficult thing, particularly when there are those who benefit from unintended consequences. Thus the regulators are left to their own devices, under the pressures of their own position as regulators, of special interests who wish to push them in one direction or another, and of the courts who may be enlisted by the special interests.

To return to the three routes by which higher education became guilty: the first route was that of its own abuses. There were two, in particular, that offered legitimate openings to correction by government. The first was discrimination on grounds of race, ethnic group, and sex. To say that higher education was guilty of such discrimination is not to accept the standard assumption—seen in so much writing on higher education today—that the guilt was widespread in 1964, when the Civil Rights Act was passed, or in 1970 and 1971, as higher education fell under regulation for affirmative action. Higher education in the South had developed in a strictly segregated fashion, with all-black and all-white colleges and universities, public and private. Whites taught in black colleges; no black was to be seen in white colleges. To what extent such discrimination was an issue in northern and western institutions in the later 1960s, whether in admission or employment, is a much disputed question. It is my impression that there was little discrimination, that for large sectors—the major sectors of higher education—the guilt of racial and ethnic and religious discrimination had in large measure passed, though admittedly many such practices had passed only recently. It is now, however, taken as a given that higher education was massively guilty. Without settling this matter, we can agree it was certainly guilty in the South, where higher education had been overtly set up on racial lines.

One can raise similar questions as to guilt for sexual discrimination. Though I tend to find the picture of higher education in the late 1960s as ridden with sexual discrimination—in admissions to undergraduate institutions, graduate programs, support for graduate students, and employment of faculty—exaggerated, there undoubtedly was some. And while it had a very different character from racial or religious discrimination (it was often thought of as benign, accommodating to women's interests and needs, regardless of how we see it now), with the radical change in women's self-image and aspirations in the late 1960s and early 1970s it was seen as offensive. Congress legislated against sex discrimination in 1972, and specifically against it in higher education (women were already protected against discrimination in employment by Title VII of the Civil Rights Act of 1964, and by the Executive Order requiring affirmative action by government contractors).

It is not unimportant, however, to determine just how guilty higher education was—or is—and how we are to assess and agree on that guilt, because it is on the assumption of guilt that the adversary stance is taken up by regulators and, more significantly, by those who spur them into action to defend minorities and women. The assessment of the extent of guilt justifies closer supervision and control. Thus, if regulators take the position that gross statistical disparities between the proportion of minorities or women enrolled in any program—or employed by an institution of higher education—and the proportions of that group in the population is a sign of either discrimination or of insufficient action to root out its vestiges, we will undoubtedly have more extensive and intrusive regulation. Such disparities do exist, and it is hard to see how they can ever fail to exist. The issue then becomes whether they are to be seen as resulting from (1) discrimination on grounds of race, ethnicity, or sex, as such, or (2) from the application of a general standard.[4]

One hopes that the struggle against the naive and mistaken view that a statistical disparity is a sign of discrimination, or of vestiges that require severe government action, is not wholly lost. In any case, whatever the conclusion of scholars as to how much discrimination existed ten years ago or how much exists today, and how present statistical disparities are to be interpreted, it is their interpretation as discrimination or something closely akin to it (structural discrimination, or vestiges, or what one will) that is the principal basis for considering higher education guilty, and that provides the wedge for the kind of regulation that is felt by higher education itself as most offensive.[5]

The second area of abuse that seems to be widely recognized in the world of post-secondary education as having justified some degree of governmental regulation is exploitation of veterans and of other students who get grants or loans for tuition from government by institutions at the fringes of higher education. I use "post-secondary education" here advisedly, because the most serious problems were not in traditional institutions of higher education, but in the area of vocational education. The enormous variety of American institutions of higher education does, of course, raise questions as to what is properly to be so considered. We are not blessed with a single national system, or with institutions that are unambiguously universities and of one kind, as are some countries. And yet, even with our great diversity, there is common recognition of what a college or university should look like or do. The enormous diversity of standards for student admission is matched by surprising homogeneity in other respects—division into courses, courses divided into departments and divisions, regular meetings, tests and grades, the accumulating of credits for certificate or degree, and the like. It is possible to accredit institutions, and private organizations have grown up to do so which consign the worst abuses (diploma on payment of fees, etc.) outside the circle of the accredited. But there were abuses.

> Among the principal offenders [of the GI Bill] were thousands of profit-making proprietary schools that sprang into existence, some of which were patronized exclusively by veterans and too many of which were found to be falsifying their records, overstating their

charges, and generally abusing the federal program. [Finn 1978:62–63]

Matters became worse with the loan programs and the massive defaults of the 1970s. What was a legitimate institution? The federal government was forced into the business of deciding. And the Veterans Administration, into the business of deciding what was legitimate academic work (Finn 1978:157–61).

But, as in the case of equal educational opportunity and affirmative action, limited abuses that could have been handled in limited ways became, in the eyes of regulators, a sign of potential universal guilt requiring sharp examination and correction. In the case of discrimination, this expansion was principally owing to the pressure of minorities and women's groups demanding stricter enforcement; in the case of veterans, it was congressional concern with the waste of government funds and the exploitation of veterans and other government-aided students. But in both cases, the forces of bureaucratic expansionism have led to the extension of the rules against abuse to the point where perfectly proper academic functions were being interfered with. The protection of veterans against exploitation leads to rules which hamper innovation. And Wayne State University finds itself subject to the rules designed to control fly-by-night proprietary institutions.

At Wayne State University [writes President Thomas N. Bonner (1979)], we are waging a fierce struggle against arbitrary and mischievous intervention by the Veterans Administration in the content and programming of a fully accredited program for veterans enrolled in our Weekend College. The V.A. has insisted that veteran students must spend twelve hours in a standard classroom each calendar week in order to qualify for full-time benefits. No matter that the total number of instructional hours for a course remains the same, the V.A. demands that we conform in every case to an 1890 conception of classroom instruction if our veterans are to receive full benefits.

The Wayne Weekend College has been accepted by national accreditation groups and by several university-wide faculty committees and has recently been commended by a UNESCO study group. Nevertheless, the V.A. continues to challenge in court the academic integrity of this and every other college and university by denying that its program constitutes full-time education in the traditional sense.

In other areas, abuse was assumed on the basis of extreme and few cases, but of course control and regulation could not limit themselves to the extreme case. All federally sponsored regulation requires controls to protect human subjects. The original intention was to protect human subjects who might be injected with drugs, or—in the worst case reported in the press—not, in order to research the effects of syphilis. Under the law of inevitable bureaucratic expansion, regulation extended from the kind of research in which subjects were injected with drugs (or not), or in which parts of their tissues were taken for examination (where the possibilities of abuse were, or course, great), to cases where human subjects were given modest tests, or asked questions, or simply observed. From a required procedure to monitor research using federal funds, the rules expanded to include all research taking place in a university, subject to the supervision of federally required institutional review boards. From research conducted by faculty and researchers, it now appears that research conducted by students as part of classwork must also be monitored. Thus, it was not only widespread abuse that led to expanded government regulation, but occasional abuse, combined with inevitable bureaucratic expansion of the scope of rules.

A second avenue to the adversary relationships between regulators and regulated in higher education was opened when universities and colleges, as employers, were covered by rules that were devised for industry and employers in general—for example, Occupational Safety and Health Administration (OSHA) rules, or the Equal Pay Act. Often rules devised for industry and full-time employment were inappropriate in some educational settings. Universities and colleges could argue, for example, that there was a difference in degree of risk associated with a certain condition when people were at work under that condition forty hours a week, and when exposure might take place only a few hours a week. The objectives of these rules (as of rules requiring equal employment, affirmative action, protection of veterans, control of abuse of federal loan and grant funds, abuse of government research funds, or of human subjects) were never at issue. But what was at issue was how the new rules to protect persons from potential abuses were devised and enforced, their heavy costs in reporting and in correcting procedures and—for OSHA and for antidiscrimination for the handicapped—in changes to physical plant. Regulations designed for industry or employers in general, when extended to colleges and universities by statute and regulation, inevitably led to some degree of adversarial relations with regulators.

Finally, there were respects in which higher education, in its specific character *as* higher education, seemed to require regulation. Here the issue was not abuse, nor the fact that higher education was inevitably blanketed in with the world of employers or business enterprises; its very essence as higher education seemed to require some degree of governmental control and to create an antagonistic relationship. Higher education typically picked and chose among applicants to undergraduate programs and to specialized graduate programs; it picked and chose among faculty, researchers, and administrators; some institutions were considered better than others, and were awarded larger shares of research funds than any formula emerging from a political process in Congress, or a rule by regulators, could justify. Higher education justified its admission policies and hiring and promotion policies by the use of standards that, in many cases, it refused to make explicit enough for regulators to police. And when it did make its standards explicit and unambiguous—e.g., for admission—it did not solve the problem but made it worse, from the point of view of regulators who wanted, for example, to see more minorities admitted or employed. Not that those who attacked higher education for refusing to be more explicit in its standards were quite honest; if the standards had indeed been more explicit, then the progress toward hiring minorities and women that government regulators wanted to see would have been even slower.

The antagonistic relationship between regulators and higher education is now fully developed. What one then *does* about regulation is another matter. One might think that there would have developed a great sense of commonality between business, laboring under its burden of rapidly increasing government regulation, and higher education, laboring under its own such burden. There has not, and there are good reasons for it. There are substantial differences in the mission and character of business and of higher education, and thus the burdens—and proper solutions—of excessive governmental regulation may be seen quite differently in the two realms. Thus, business is most afflicted by environmental regulation—which hampers expansion, which mandates extremely heavy expenditures, and which may impose differential burdens on different parts of the same industry. Occupational safety and health regulations impose, perhaps, a similar burden. Affirmative action and equal opportunity are serious problems, but business and industry are aided in dealing with them by the fact that (1) they are hierarchically organized, and new procedures to come into compliance with given government rules are more easily instituted; (2) since hierarchy is the expected organizational pattern, there is less occasion for rebellion in the ranks; (3) business and industry are used to hiring by the numbers (tests), because so many enterprises are very large, and they hire and promote many people for essentially similar tasks. While it may be offensive to managers to adjust the numbers to reflect race, ethnicity, and sex, what is required is simply adjustment rather than totally new procedures. Business is, for the most part, spared from the entire complex of rules and regulations required by various types of aid to students in post-secondary education—determining who gets aid, reporting, monitoring, and the like. It is also, for the most part, freed from the requirements for the protection of human subjects in research. Research is, in any case, a much smaller part of business activity, and less of it is federally funded. (Admittedly, if these requirements apply to all research conducted by any government contractor, all business research is covered, too; but while non–federally funded research is now reviewed by institutional review boards (IRBs), this authority does not flow from a blanket requirement that federal contractors establish IRBs.)

The differences are thus extensive. As against the priority taken by environmental protection and occupational safety and health regulation for business, higher education finds as its most difficult regulatory problems, as we indicated above, affirmative action and equal opportunity in employment, the associated issue (only now beginning to fall under government regulation) of autonomy in making decisions on admission, and the protection of human subjects in research. Since higher education is, in any case, not expanding and hardly polluting, the environmental issues are not severe; though Harvard University, to its chagrin, found that one of the mechanisms for delay imposed by unsympathetic neighbors—that eventually lost it the Kennedy Library—was the requirement for an environmental impact statement.

Higher education not only finds that federal regulation affects it differently. Spokesmen for higher education have argued that it is so different that the burden of regulation, which may quite properly be imposed on profit-oriented business and industry, should be, for higher education, eased or lifted entirely because of its distinctive characteristics.

There have been two kinds of arguments for the position that higher education deserves different considerations when government regulates. The first is basically an economic argument. Because higher education is non–profit-making, and because of some special economic characteristics as an enterprise, it has particular difficulties in dealing with the costs of government regulation.

The second argument is very different. It is that higher education, because of its functions, is very different from business. The functions of teaching, research, and preserving and extending a cultural and scientific heritage place it in a very different position from the purely economic institutions of a society, and for this reason must be exempted from many of the regulations imposed by government. The claim, in effect, is that higher education is something like a church. And the church is not only exempt from paying taxes, as is higher education, but may even get a special exemption from those government regulations that are most heavily invested with moral content, such as the prohibition of discrimination on the basis of race, ethnicity, and national origin (this exemption for religious institutions is written into Title VII—the equal employment title—of the Civil Rights Act of 1964). Both arguments have some merit. In the end, neither will, I suspect, do much to differentiate higher education from business in the minds of congressmen, the executive branch, or the bureaucracy. Let us consider whether they should.

The first argument is well presented in the first major study of the costs of government regulation. Van Alstyne and Coldren (1976) studied the costs of implementing federally mandated social programs for universities and colleges, and limited themselves to those costs that were imposed on universities and colleges in their capacity as business enterprises. They took a sample of six institutions, and asked them to estimate the costs of implementing programs requiring equal employment opportunity, affirmative action, equal pay, no age discrimination, occupational safety and health, environmental protection, fair wage and hour standards, contributions for unemployment compensation, social security taxes, retirement benefit standards, and a few others. Some of these programs (e.g., social security, unemployment insurance) do not involve any federal regulation, as we understood it; they can be managed simply through bookkeeping. This may make them costly indeed, but they involve little in the way of *regulation*. Thus, the fact that institutions of higher education must contribute to the social security accounts of their employees or must contribute for unemployment insurance funds, and that social security taxes have been undergoing a rapid increase, impose strictly financial costs and in no way infringe on any distinctive function of a university or college. The affirmative action requirements, of course, do go directly to the question of appointments of individuals and their qualifications, and thus are in a separate category. One might argue that occupational safety and health requirements designed for industry bear particularly harshly on teaching and research laboratories; that requirements for modifying the physical characteristics of buildings to accommodate the handicapped (not covered in this early study) are particularly hard on colleges and universities which have characteristically grown up over many years and were not designed for the convenient management of materials—as industrial and even commercial buildings have been—which means they are also convenient for wheelchairs (large and heavy elevators, or built on one level without steps).

Van Alstyne and Coldren look upon universities and colleges as economic enterprises, and consider the distinctive economic impact of federal regulations on such enterprises. And they do find, from this limited perspective, a distinctive burden borne by institutions of higher education. (1) Colleges and universities are bound for a year by early announced tuition fees, which they cannot alter in response to higher costs imposed by government programs. (2) Because of tenure and long-range employment contracts, they have less opportunity to respond rapidly to increases in costs resulting from new federal programs. (3) Since they are not as centralized as business—indeed, are highly decentralized—the costs of communicating the details of federal requirements throughout the institution are greater. (4) While private profit-making business gets most of its income from setting prices, and these can be varied with costs to some extent, the equivalent in higher education to price-setting is setting tuition charges, and these cover only part of income. Nothing can be done to raise income from endowment in response to higher costs of federal regulation, and not much can be done to get more from the federal government and state government programs of research support, student aid, and general support, simply because higher costs are imposed by other federal programs. (5) When private industry cannot shift costs, at least its tax burden is reduced, so it is not bearing 100 percent of the costs of increased regulation, while higher education, not paying income taxes, does bear 100 percent. (6) Because higher education is more labor intensive than most private business, social program costs, which are related to the number of employees, are more onerous for them. And the rising dependence of the federal government on payroll taxes, which all enterprises pay, as against income taxes, which only profit-making enterprises pay, means a higher proportionate financial burden on higher education.

All true. One suspects that many branches of private business could also make arguments as to the special burdens that are imposed on *them* due to the distinctive character of their business. But is the academic enterprise *as such* hobbled? Aside from the discrimination statutes and regulations, it is hard to see how, except in the very general sense that the costs of federal programs and regulations inevitably mean less money devoted to educational innovation. This is one of the arguments made in a study of the impact of federal regulations at the University of Iowa (Spriestersbach and Farrell 1977:27–30). Every industry is differentially affected by federal regulations and programs, and can make a claim it could perform its function "better" if this differential impact were reduced. Thus, the bus companies argue that gasoline taxes burden them especially, and the railroads, that maintaining their own right of way burdens them especially, and both tell us we would have better service if federal taxes and subsidies were arranged to take this into account.

It is valid to point out the distinctive economic characteristics of higher education as an enterprise, as it is valid to defend the interests of each industry as it is differentially affected by government regulation, and as it is valid for cities and regions to demonstrate the differential impact of what are expected to be fair burdens, or fairly distributed relief. The solution in this case is also clear: more money from the federal government for higher education, so it can shoulder the additional burden of government regulation without harm to educational and research functions.

This is a popular response, of course, and many see it as the main answer to the complaints of higher education. Thus, Stephen Bailey (1978:111), one of the most informed and perceptive analysts of the relationships of the federal government with higher education, writes:

> Government must be aware of the special financial burdens on colleges and universities that accompany compliance with new laws and regulations. . . . It is not unreasonable for higher education to request government assistance in meeting some of the administrative costs imposed by new government mandates.

And this is the view, too, of Carol van Alstyne (1978:117), who writes:

> Now, in general, we accept the contention that the regulations do apply to higher education, but if they apply, then there are costs of meeting them which must be met. . . . Those who have written the laws and are applying them are beginning to recognize there are indeed costs involved in implementing these regulations, but then they argue that the higher education community must bear those costs, just as does any other enterprise.

Dr. van Alstyne argues that our position should be that "the nonprofit educational enterprises are less able to recover those costs than are profit-oriented firms."

This seems an easy solution to the problem of federal regulations, easy enough in principle, certainly, even if difficult in execution. It requires good information, well-staffed roof organizations in Washington, good lobbying. It is understandable that it is one of the main conclusions to emerge from studies of the problem of federal regulations by those presently and formerly on the staff of the American Council on Education. It seems futile to them, I assume, to press the rather stronger second position on why higher education is different, either because they doubt Congress will buy it, or perhaps because they do not buy it themselves.

This second and more interesting basis for the claim that higher education is different from profit-oriented business is that it is not only an industry with special economic characteristics, but that its essential functions are very different from and—one cannot avoid the presumption or implication in this argument—higher than simply providing automobiles or toothpaste. The search for truth itself does seem a higher objective than most we can think of. The transmission of truth also qualifies. And yet, despite my respect for this argument, one wonders if it will stand up politically—where it must—with congressmen, their staffs, key lobbyists, and the media. Are there functions in higher education that are unique to it and of the highest value, and are they indeed distorted and withered as federal regulation grows? Are there damages endured by the educational enterprise that are not to be assuaged solely by money?

This was the debate that ensued when the University Centers for Rational Alternatives conducted a conference on the problem of government and higher education in 1976 (Hook, Kurz, Todorovich 1978). A variety of positions was presented. At one end of the spectrum were those who saw only positive results from federal regulation, and who interpreted the attack on government regulation as a conservative, or reactionary, or indeed, racist resistance to its clearly progressive objectives. In the middle were those who accepted the objectives but were overwhelmed by the costs and problems of regulation. Better administration by the federal government, and more money to assist in complying with regulations, seemed to be the answer. At the other end of the spectrum were those who argued that the distinctive functions for higher education were being seriously damaged, and that money would not help. Another key axis of disagreement was on the question of whether higher education was like or unlike other regulated institutions. But there was a sharp division among those who argued it was like other institutions. To Kenneth Tollett, higher education was guilty of racism, as was, of course, the rest of American society; all should thus be subject to the strong discipline of government regulation. To Robert Bork, too, higher education could not expect special treatment from government; but he argued that just as higher education was harmed by government regulation, so, too, was business. They were the same, in that higher education could not expect different treatment from that accorded business, and the same, too, in that their *distinctive* and *different* functions—research and education for higher education, production of goods and services for business—were hobbled by the growth of government and by the steady imposition of governmental objectives on all *autonomous* institutions of society.

I believe Bork set the problem properly. Higher education is in many ways the same as any other kind of enterprise. If society sets for all of them a requirement that employees must be protected from unemployment, illness, indigency in old age, or that they must not be discriminated against on grounds of race, ethnicity, sex, handicap, age, then higher education cannot reasonably demand an exception. Those who emphasize the inner core of higher education, the search for truth and its transmission, can make a claim for exemption from some government regulation on these grounds, similar to the claim one would make for a church. But higher education is implicated in so many other things that it cannot succeed in making the claim good. Governmental rules should apply to all, in their capacities as employers, or as builders and maintainers of physical facilities. The complaint that it costs too much is the lesser complaint, and can be managed by adding more staff, more lawyers, more lobbyists.

But there still remains the inner distinctive core, the teaching and research function at its best. And there *is* a best, where teachers and students feel that their relationship is not one that is bound by contract and susceptible of having its claims tested in administrative tribunals and courts outside the university and college, and where researchers feel that they are engaged in a distinctive autonomous search that is hampered when they are treated as contractors.

In its public face, higher education is like any other enterprise that uses buildings, hires employees, signs contracts; if it demands exemption, it will not get very far. In its inner face, it is very different indeed. But, in saying that, I do not deny that *any* kind of enterprise is ''different indeed'' from others, and I put aside the question—for the purpose of this chapter—of whether these functions must be ordered in a hierarchy of worth or value. The problem is that the two faces are closely interconnected, and the inner face is damaged as the outer face complies with federal regulation. I am convinced of the damage. Even those who tell us that higher education can live quite comfortably with government regulation alarm us in their prescriptions as to how this alliance is to be managed. Thus, Ernest Gellhorn (Dean, Arizona State University College of Law) and Barry B. Boyer (Associate Dean, Faculty of Law and Jurisprudence, SUNY-Buffalo), who think the problem is much exaggerated, tell us that we have transitional growing pains. ''In large measure they can be traced to conditions such as understaffing in the regulatory agency, and enforcement officials' unfamiliarity with the operations and mores of the university.'' The prescription thus seems to be more bureaucrats who are more familiar with how universities work. The universities and colleges should themselves become more political and litigious, and should affect the regulatory process. The roof organization of higher education must, of course, be strengthened to deal with the increased number of knowledgeable regulators (Gellhorn and Boyer 1978:46, 49).

> [A] single, central association can develop influence and resources that its dispersed members can rarely match. With a full-time specialized staff, the association can master the intricacies of regulatory programs more completely than an administrator or manager who devotes only part of his or her attention to the task.

Not that the college or university administrator can thereby rest easy, knowing his Washington roof organization is on the job. He has quite a job, too. Charles B. Saunders, Jr. (1976:223), Vice President for Governmental Relations, American Council on Education, gives the new job description that will help the roof organization domesticate the regulators:

> Whether planning legal, political, or administrative action, however, the basic need is for better information from the individual campus to make the case for higher education. We need a moratorium on indignant rhetoric and vague laments that government will be the death of us. Instead we need facts and careful analysis.
>
> What federal programs cause the greatest problem on *your* campus? Precisely how and why? Are the problems growing, and are the types of problems changing? What are the trends? Can you document increases in indirect costs resulting from federal reporting and record-keeping requirements? What specific steps would you recommend to reduce the costs and administrative burdens of federal programs? What specific changes would you suggest in the wording of federal regulations? Have you analyzed the latest proposed regulations for agency programs which affect your campus, and have you shared the issues you identified with your associations and your congressman as well as the offending agency?
>
> These are the kinds of questions that must be asked and that individual institutions must answer for the higher education community to make an effective case for continued progress in deregulation.

The job description necessary to live comfortably with regulation becomes even more alarming in the proposals of Alfred D. Sumberg (1978:78–79), Director of Government Relations, American Association of University Professors:

> The Office of Education estimates that it will take about three dozen sets of regulations to interpret and implement the funded programs under the education amendments [of 1976]. Eight of those proposed regulations have already been published; four were published in the Federal Register of April 8. There will be public hearings at various locations around the country, and there will be ample opportunity to comment on the proposed regulations in detail either at the hearings

> or in writing. Those proposed regulations require careful reading at the campus level and should be read in the context of experiences with those programs on the campus. Both written comments and oral testimony are carefully considered by the appropriate officials of the Office of Education and frequently revision is necessary prior to the issuance of final regulations. If past practice is followed, however, there will be only a handful of comments and little testimony submitted. Then at some later day, faculty and campus administrators will find themselves in conflict with some provision of the final regulations and they will wonder openly and articulately about how the regulations were drafted. . . .
>
> . . . [W]hen reading proposed regulations, one should analyze carefully the legislation and its legislative history, including committee reports and the debates on the floors of the House and Senate.

One wonders, after all this, what else is a college administrator expected to do?

It is not only that living comfortably with regulators requires turning college administrators into monitors of federal legislation and regulation, and researchers into the impact of federal regulation on their campus. It also means increasing the power of central Washington organizations, since only they will really understand what is going on, when to act, how to act, and who is to be influenced. It also means increasing the power of central administrators of traditionally decentralized institutions. The regulators are already very annoyed that college presidents and deans cannot simply give orders, the way corporation presidents can. And indeed, presidents and deans are desperately trying to find ways to achieve the results regulators want, even in the absence of the power to give orders. They can require so many reports and justifications for the hiring of what is called a "majority male" that chairmen are relieved when they can appoint a minority or a woman.[6]

All these results follow from laws or regulations whose objectives seem entirely desirable, and which address themselves, it would appear, only to the public—and quite legitimately regulatable—face of higher education. But the fact is that not only do the legitimate actions of regulations change—for the worse—the college and university by overemphasizing its administration, and overemphasizing within administration the task of dealing with regulation and the roles of lawyers and litigators, but there also seems no way of keeping much of the regulation dealing with the public face from infringing on the private face. Who can object to the Equal Pay Act, which requires that men and women receive the same pay for the same work? But then the Department of Labor will insist on defining what is the "same work," in which presumably they will weigh the quality of research and teaching—something they have no capacity to do. Estelle Fishbein's (1978:62–63) account of their operations against Northeastern University is alarming:

The Department of Labor has never issued regulations or guidelines regarding the application of the Equal Pay Act to faculty pay in higher education. No definitive policy statement has ever been issued. This, however, has not prevented the Department of Labor from bringing suit against Northeastern University, charging violation of the Equal Pay Act. The complaint filed in federal court by the government is skeletal and conclusory despite the fact that it followed a two-year investigation. Finally, the department selected fifty-seven cases of alleged sex discrimination in salary levels, not one of which involved alleged inequity within the university's academic departmental structure. Labor is apparently contending that it can select matchmates for female faculty members across department lines (one professor being likened to another), although nowhere has any statute or regulation given notice to universities that faculty in all departments must be paid the same, nor has any definitive policy statement been issued from the department setting forth criteria to be used in equating faculty in the various disciplines. Quite recently the American Council on Education demanded of the Department of Labor, under authority of the Freedom of Information Act, the Department's policy memoranda and instructions to its enforcement personnel concerning application of the Equal Pay Act to faculty employees in universities; the Council also sought reports of all studies dealing with the application of the Act. The Department's reply indicated there were no documents of such a nature. Nevertheless, Northeastern University, in its negotiation of an out of court settlement, is being asked by the government for a consent decree that would include an admission of discrimination.

One other note on the possible damage that regulation inflicts: it is much more evident to those at the working face of education—teachers and researchers—than it is to administrators. This is understandable. The administrators—in contact with regulators, regulations, their own staffs of lawyers and affirmative action officers attempting to bring the institution into compliance, burdened with the responsibility for budgets and the future of the institution—see more ways of adapting the institution to regulatory needs than do teachers and researchers. Undoubtedly the latter have their own blind spots, since they do not have administrative responsibilities. But they see and feel the harm more strongly when they must comply with new regulations and requirements in conducting research, in hiring new faculty, and—perhaps eventually—in preparing and conducting classes. (The regulations for the handicapped suggest they should make an effort to adapt their teaching to the needs of the variously handicapped who do not have normal auditory, visual, and speech faculties [Bailey 1978:51–52]—an entering wedge?)

On this difference in perception between faculty when they undertake regulatory tasks and faculty when they act as researchers, a study of a sample of sixty-one institutional review boards passing on research involving human subjects is particularly revealing. Only 13 percent of the review board members from the biomedical sciences and 11 percent of the review board members from the behavioral and social sciences agreed with the statement, "The review procedure is an unwarranted intrusion on an investigator's autonomy—at least to some extent." Much higher percentages of research investigators agreed—25 and 38 percent of biomedical scientists and behavioral and social scientists, respectively. Presented with the statement, "The review committee gets into areas which are not appropriate to its functions—at least to some extent," 39 percent of the biomedical review board members, 23 percent of those from the behavioral and social sciences, agreed. Their colleagues, who were trying to get their research projects through, agreed in much higher percentages—50 and 49 percent (Gray, Cooke, Tannenbaum 1978:1100). What is intriguing in these results, of course, is that there are faculty members on both sides of this divide; but place a man in the position of a regulator and he is likely to see his task as more important, his role as less intrusive, the extension of his role as more justified, than those he regulates.

There *is* a problem with the federal regulation of higher education. It is a problem that is not going to be settled by simply adjusting to regulation, because regulation inevitably and insistently begins to involve itself more and more with the functions of higher education that it considers crucial, and for good reason. Let us acknowledge that much of higher education is far from the pure-minded search for truth and its transmission, that research is often dominated by funding opportunities (which doesn't necessarily make it bad or unnecessary research), that teaching is often a rather journeyman exercise, engaged in without passion by teachers and accepted for purposes of a proper credential by students. But a very large number of institutions of higher education do preserve its essential character, and large numbers of administrators and faculty are engaged in protecting and carrying out these functions. Autonomy in the decisions as to what scholars to employ, what research enterprises to pursue, what students to admit, and how to teach them, seems to me the essential prerequisite for preserving the inner functions of higher education. And yet it is just these autonomous functions that federal regulation increasingly finds as irritating obstacles to carrying out ends set, sometimes by Congress, and more often by federal employees operating under the influence of pressure groups representing one or another organized sector of the population, and appealing to the courts to impose their view of the proper function of regulation upon federal agencies.

The most drastic example to date of federal intervention in the autonomous affairs of universities is to be found in the *Adams v. Richardson* (now *Adams v. Califano*) litigation, under which the NAACP is requiring the Department of Health, Education, and Welfare (HEW) to restructure higher education in the Southern states which, in the past, imposed and maintained segregated institutions. This litigation now requires these states to achieve certain proportions of white and black students in given institutions of higher education, and gives the Office of Civil Rights the opportunity to judge the legitimacy of placing educational programs and faculties at different locations from the point of view of their presumed impact on education.[7]

But what is to be done? I have rejected, on principled grounds, the argument that higher education will manage well enough as the regulators and regulated get to know each other better, and as the government is persuaded to kick in some money to help institutions of higher education with the added costs. Of course, more money will permit Northeastern to raise the wages of its female faculty to what the Wages and Hours Division considers appropriate; it will not solve the problem of who is to judge the qualifications and worth of faculty, and determine what differential rewards are just and proper. Of course, more money will help North Carolina solve the problem of moving its programs and facilities from one campus or another to comply with HEW's and the judge's mandate as to how to achieve a better racial balance between institutions; but it will not solve the problem of who is to determine the mission of different educational institutions and their programs and needs in the light of a distinctive mission. (And in the latter case it is even doubtful that, with all the coerced goodwill in the world, the factors that lead blacks to choose one institution of higher education differentially, whites to choose another, can really be managed—whether by courts, HEW, the state systems, or the individual institutions. And when the expected results are not forthcoming, the stage will be set for more intrusive intervention.)[8]

I have also rejected, on principled grounds, the argument that higher education should be exempt. I do not believe we should accept the position that higher education must not suffer from insensitive and crude regulatory policies, but that business and industry may.[9] Higher education should argue that all institutions should be freed from the illegitimate expansion of governmental power, and from its unnecessary intrusion into the workings of autonomous institutions. Business should argue the same. And both should use their influence and resources to restrict regulation to its legitimate objectives.

It may be properly asked, do these general terms have any explicit meaning, or do they simply say, in disguised language, that higher education and industry alike should resist fairness for minorities, women, the handicapped? This general prescription can be made concrete, and without infringing on fairness, justice, or compassion. There is a sharp and radical difference between nondiscrimination (as required in federal legislation) and affirmative action (as required of government contractors), and the insistence by regulatory bodies that population representation is the measure of absence of discrimination, and that all contractors must set up goals that are, in effect, quotas. There is a sharp and radical difference between employing the handicapped and admitting them to institutions of higher education without discrimination, as Congress commanded, and extending the definition of the handicapped to include drug addicts and alcoholics, as the regulations written by HEW require. These are examples of an illegitimate bureaucratic expansionism in areas distinctively crucial for higher education. I have no doubt there are similar examples in areas of regulation particularly crucial for business.

I have argued earlier that there is an inevitable tendency for regulation to expand—to do more than Congress requires, more than the executive requires, more even than the written regulation requires. This tendency for regulation to expand is based on a new "iron triangle." The old iron triangle of the regulatory agency, the regulated industry, and the congressional oversight committee in the past led regulations to become protective of the regulated. The new triangle of the outside, well-organized, special interest, the regulating agency, and the court now move in the opposite direction—the regulating agencies become enemies of the institutions they regulate. It is this that must be contested. And it will not be contested well if higher education takes the pusillanimous and immoral position that it's all right for you to do it to them—just don't do it to us.

7

PAUL SEABURY

Epilogue—a Final Footnote

A young Pig was shut up in a fold yard with a Goat and a Sheep. On one occasion when the shepherd laid hold of him, he grunted and squealed and resisted violently. The Sheep and the Goat complained of his distressing cries, saying, "He often handles us, and we do not cry out." To this the Pig replied, "Your handling and mine are very different things. He catches you only for your wool, or your milk, but he lays hold on me for my very life."

Aesop's Fables

This pig tried to distinguish his plight from that of his companions in the fold yard. If, for our purposes, he is the American businessman, the lamb has been the American professor—at least, until recently. The good shepherd indeed cares for him, cards his wool, shields him from the wolves, and makes him to lie down in green pastures. But recently the shepherd has been seen reading recipes for *shish kebab*.

Ten years ago, had the subject of government control of universities been discussed among tormented academics, the most plausible apocalyptic vision then would have included national guard encampments, legislative investigations, stormy show-trials of campus activists, punitive reprisals against university budgets by outraged lawmakers, and so on. Crystal balls are best at showing—or caricaturing—what we know is happening now. They often miss the underlying tendencies of things.

The essays in this book have shown a very different, but very real, picture. The federal regulatory mode, in its infancy a decade ago with respect to universities, oddly enough did *not* commence—as did federal regulation of business corporations—in a climate of suspicion and animosity. Universities were *not* charged by Washington lawmakers and rulemakers with being malefactors of great wealth, social predators, or ruthless exploiters of the masses. At the time, they were not even charged (a more credible accusation, under the circumstances) with being centers of subversion and ideological intimidation. The regulations flowered in consequence of a benign beneficence which soon made the university dependent on an admiring benefactor. When, in the early 1970s, the regulatory process commenced in earnest, legislators and bureaucrats looked upon these institutions as intrinsically valuable, and as worthy of continued—if not increased—support. So valuable were they that they could be regarded as key social laboratories in which a new and better generation of Americans could be raised. The gentle hand of the State could ease this process of improvement along by making these institutions more accessible and open—more humane, less hazardous to life and limb, more egalitarian, more responsible in their conception of the social consequences of their research, and so on.

In this, we discern a marked contrast of the early attitude towards these new objects of governmental control, and the early punitive attitudes taken by lawmakers and rulemakers towards institutions of business and finance. Yet starting from quite different attitudinal points, the federal regulation of business and university today has ended up in similar quagmires of adversarial frustration and resentment. In both instances, we notice that—wholly apart from the monumental and commonly shared difficulties with paper work and compliance—the worlds of business and university both experience a massive loss of autonomy as actors in a once-free society.

We need measuring devices to ascertain where our universities stand, and to measure the speed and direction by which the momentum of change impels us. Horror stories echo through faculty clubs and campus administrations, but they do not necessarily elicit understanding or sympathy from outsiders. One is reminded, in this respect, of the sage words of a man who encountered an old friend one day on the street. The friend asked, "And how is your wife?" The man replied, "Compared to what?"

Richard Lyman has pointed out, in Chapter 3, that how we compare our current situation does make a difference. Do we compare our condition with the regulatory status of universities in the totalitarian world? Then we can be overjoyed at our good fortune. This first generation of university regulators at least refrains from penetrating the central core of teaching and scholarship in order to direct what is fitting for students and scholars to learn and to teach. The regulatory reach into faculty research thus far has been largely confined to laboratory work and federally supported scientific research; here it is motivated less by political concerns than by considerations—however justified in individual cases—of safety, accountability, and protection of subjects. The hand of the federal government *thus far* has not intruded itself into the inner constitutional order of universities, as has long been the case in continental European countries, to determine how and by whom basic educational decisions are made.

The U.S. professoriate is not appointed by Ministries of Education and Culture, nor are curricula inspected and approved by government agencies. Oddly enough, and characteristic perhaps of the current situation, the most frequently heard complaint from administrators about the federal government is not the paranoid lament about Big Brother, but rather about having to deal with a myriad of interested, pestering federal authorities, each of which in its own way seeks to become a chef in the academic kitchen. Ironically, of course, one way to ease such complaints about too many cooks would be to *concentrate and rationalize* federal authority—a development which might conjure up an adversary far more formidable and purposeful than those which universities now confront. It might even be called a Department of Education—and, not surprisingly, steps are being taken in Congress to see that it will soon come into being.

We can take less comfort when we look, not sideways into academic folkways elsewhere in the world, but backwards, to see whence we have come in such a short time. It is the very *speed* at which U.S. universities have moved from there to here which causes the greatest surprise. If the momentum continues at its present pace, we may surmise that we are not far removed from a time when the regulatory propensity will have extended its reach deep into our porous institution from the beachheads which it now occupies. The story which this book tells goes back only to the 1960s—less than one generation; before that time, we notice a condition of freedom which now is almost unrecognizable.

The laments most often heard within the American academic community chiefly come from administrators; it is their responsibility to cope with this surge of federal authority. But, as Robert Sproull's chapter eloquently illustrates, the next most serious complaints come from scientific researchers and experimentalists whose mode and climate of work have been severely impaired. Scholars in the social sciences and humanities have been less directly affected by these developments in their work, but there is no reason to suppose that this must remain true. Their ability to initiate appointments of new colleagues has been gravely impaired by "affirmative action."

As this book goes to press, there now are more signs that the federal regulators intend to enlarge the scope of their intervention on two widely separated fronts: college athletic programs, and what is now called "research on human subjects." Since neither of these matters has been dealt with in preceding chapters, I feel that at least some reference should be made to them.

Some academics, to be sure, today may not agree either with Plato or with contemporary sports devotees that athletics should constitute a legitimate part of a college program. But it *is* a recognized and traditional feature of most U.S. colleges and universities. And as such, it also is now subject to the meticulous and heavy-handed control of Washington officials. Here the egalitarian regulatory intent is to be observed in a current HEW attempt to either eliminate distinctions between ("segregated"!) men's and women's sports, or to require colleges meticulously to equalize expenditures on them so that they will be proportional to the number of men and women engaging in athletics. Thus, substantially equal per capita expenditures are demanded for athletic scholarships, recruitment, equipment and supplies, travel and publicity. The salaries for men's and women's coaches are also to be equalized.

As the *Wall Street Journal* pointed out ("Block That Kick," 12 April 1979), these athletic guidelines are likely to severely damage college sports. The federal accounting system, for instance, measures only college *expenditures* for highly expensive intercollegiate sports like basketball and football, while ignoring the large revenues these bring in—revenues which, in turn, help finance other parts of the athletic program. As a natural consequence of equalization, expenditures on men's football teams would be greatly reduced in all but rich colleges, and thus, ineluctably, the amount of income from them, as well as their intermural competitiveness, would be sharply reduced. In this, as in other federal regulations, there is a seeming blindness to the incalculable costs and side damages of abstract, single-minded reforms.

Many scholars may be indifferent to football, but, to paraphrase Daniel Webster in the *Dartmouth College* case, "It may be a big sport, sir, but there are those who love it."

In the instance, however, of federal regulation of research on human subjects, we see a very different monitory intention—not to equalize, but to reduce or abolish risk to persons who are the objects of research. Federal regulators, again via HEW, now intend to enlarge the scope of such regulation to include not merely the biological, medical, and behavioral sciences—already subject to such controls—but the social sciences and humanities as well. If, as appears likely, HEW promulgates its new regulations governing "risks to human subjects"—another project of the Guardian Democracy—university research review boards will be federally obliged to scrutinize and approve and police *all* campus research proposals with human beings as their subjects, to ascertain *in advance* whether the consequences of such research may pose harm to persons or groups of persons. Presumably, historians will be least affected, since most of their subjects do not belong to the land of the living. Only their reputations are susceptible to harm. In such a fashion, a doctrine of prior restraint upon scholarship comes into being, *for the best of intentions*. In this instance as in all the others, the threat of contract cancellation is at hand as the ultimate weapon. Universities are the government's contractors; if the government wishes to dismiss them for not doing its bidding, what recourse have they?

One does not have to be a libertarian or a defender of absolute university autonomy to realize the danger which such regulations pose to the vital activities of universities and scholars. It might be supposed that, were such a doctrine of prior restraint promulgated on the American Fourth Estate—and for exactly the same benign purposes—an immediate consequence would be a tumult the likes of which have not been heard since the *New York Times*–Ellsberg case. But universities are not newspapers; newspapers do not get federal government handouts. The government does not endow them or hire them to do its work. The U.S. government does not ration newsprint among them—once a favorite trick of the Peron and Allende regimes. The American press has not made a habit of responding timorously to such intrusions. But the prudential mode is one which harassed university administrators are likely to adopt—and for very good reason. As a legal counsel for one major university recently wrote, in an *aide-mémoire* to his chief:

> DHEW might not take lightly the University's refusal to comply with the regulation even if it was acting on the advice of counsel that the regulation is most likely invalid. The competition for research dollars is so great that DHEW could "punish" the University through mechanisms over which the University would have no redress. Furthermore, we are presently embroiled in various disputes with DHEW and it is possible that further University "obstreperousness" in one area might have an effect on DHEW's decisions in other areas.

Sound advice. Such risks are very real. At the University of California this year, the principled and stubborn refusal of the university to release confidential personnel correspondence of certain departments to HEW inspectors (and then, of course, through the Freedom of Information Act, *urbi et orbi*) led to explicit threats of federal contract termination—in this case, concretely, termination of vital and delicate laboratory research in the biological sciences, in no way involved in the flap over confidentiality. In this illustrative case, had university public health researchers been dismissed and their facilities shut down, including a vital cell culture laboratory, basic long-term research on botulinal toxins, on San Joaquin Valley Fever, and on other diseases to man and beast would have come to an abrupt halt. This threat, incidentally, has not—at this writing—been rescinded. It does not take much imagination to realize that the "human risk" implicit in such blackmail transcends the career prospects and livelihood of the thirty-six laboratory scientists and their graduate students. The case is still in the courts.

But to return to the "human subjects" issue: we already have institutional review boards on campus which, presumably, as federal agents, will henceforth screen proposals to see that they comply with the arbitrary whims of government functionaries. The General Counsel of the Johns Hopkins University writes,[1]

> The interplay between the national bureaucratic tendencies of government auditory bodies, granting agencies and their functionaries makes the evolution of the IRB (institutional review board) as a "highly efficient *in terrorem* mechanism" highly probable.

Some sophisticated defenders of the U.S. university stress the unwisdom of trying to make a special case for higher education's exemption from federal rules which apply also to other institutions, such as business firms. In one important sense, they are right. To engage in special pleading for exemption on grounds of the "unique" character of higher education is not likely to gain many friends. The "not us, we are different!" argument will not carry much weight with the man in the street, nor with the regulators themselves, and it is certain to arouse wry amusement among higher education's natural allies in the business community. The argument resembles a dubious proposition put forward a decade or less ago by a distinguished American scholar when race-quota hiring was being first pressed upon colleges and universities. It was all right, he argued, for *all those other* lesser colleges and state universities—but not for us! Spare us! If racial quotas are applied to *us* as well as to *them,* this will fatally damage the quality scholarship which *we* engage in.

Regardless of other considerations, such as the principle of logical consistency, such a snobbish stand is strategically self-defeating—any principled resistance to outrageous regulatory demands requires the broadest possible coalition of forces. To seek to protect only the presumptively "best" from the fantasies of a federally administered "equality of results" program is akin to claiming the right to make "triage" decisions on the battlefield when oneself is wounded. What, in fact, such an argument ignores, moreover, is the very possibility that many among the bureaucratic "equalizers" have been particularly inspired to fulfill their egalitarian ambitions precisely in the most meritocratic institutions.[2]

Yet despite all this, a special case must be advanced with respect to the interests of the American university. The example has to be made precisely because this otherwise abstract issue cannot be understood by the public. The case cannot rest upon a principled and absolute claim for autonomy. Outside observers with reasonable powers of memory have no difficulty in remembering the "pigs off campus" chants of academic ideologues—including not a few faculty members—when many universities were recently convulsed with internal attacks upon their integrity. No demonstrably corrupt or internally threatened institution in a civilized society can expect that its autonomy will be respected by outsiders, especially by the State; the claim to autonomy is valid only to the extent that the university demonstrate its institutional commitment to valid goals in the pursuit of learning and teaching. We know from intimate experience and from observing universities in other settings—Latin America, in particular—that the cry for autonomy too often has come from within the university by those who have wished to make it a siege fortress for political movements. Even universities can degenerate into chaos or fall prey to petty tyrannies. In this, they are not exempt from the general laws of human nature. Academic freedom, like the ideas of a free press or freedom of religion, is not an absolute right. It remains valid only when its practitioners are committed to its essential and express tasks.

Another consideration: qualities which may be virtues in politics can be vices for scholarship, and the other way around. The fashionable political virtues reflected in the new regulators' directives are bent upon achieving an egalitarian society which is simultaneously a humane society and an environmentally risk-free society. Universities, as well as business firms, are deemed to be vessels within which these admirable goals are to be achieved under the close scrutiny of public officials. Oddly enough, while their means are very different, the goals of student militants in the 1960s bear some resemblance to the current goals of the new regulators—and, of course, a strong possibility exists that there is considerable overlap between the two groups. The students, in their time, wished the university to be the *agent* to revolutionize society; the regulators now wish the university to be a *laboratory* for social change. The difference lies in the source from which the orders come. But in either case, what is required of the university is that it assign to such a social role a priority which directly conflicts with essential and central tasks.

Scholarship and learning cherish novelty, achievement, and pride of authorship and accomplishment. Ward Elliott has pointed out, in his *Rise of the Guardian Democracy* (1974:154–55), that the best scholarship prizes also the abstract and timeless over the immediate and the concrete. For good reason, one should fear the consequences of a *sophistocracy*—government by scholars. As Elliott points out, the scholarly preferences, "which are well-suited for expanding and sharpening knowledge, are ruinous for democratic politics, which depend for their operability on consensus, consultation and compromise, and on the exclusion from their agenda of issues which are needlessly divisive." By the same token, we must fear as well the control of scholars by political governors. In the words of the late Justice Felix Frankfurter (1957), concurring in a Supreme Court case touching on the integrity of universities:

> These pages need not be burdened with proof, based on the testimony of a cloud of witnesses, of the dependence of a free society on free universities. This means the exclusion of governmental intervention in the intellectual life of the university. It matters little whether such intervention occurs avowedly or through action that inevitably tends to check the ardor and fearlessness of scholars, qualities at once so fragile and indispensable for fruitful academic labor.

NOTES

1. Paul Seabury: "The Advent of the Academic Bureaucrats"

1. One consequence of this, as far as the nation's capital is concerned, is that until recently the universities in Washington were distinctly second rate, and they still do not rank high in the pecking order of U.S. higher education. In the continental European tradition of education, this would appear incredible.
2. At UC–Berkeley, the famous "loyalty oath" controversy of the late 1940s is a classic example of this tension. The university president, Robert Gordon Sproul, anxious to shield the institution against legislative intrusions, devised an innocuous "oath" which professors would take as a substitute for a more onerous one concocted by a zealous state legislature. Sproul's strategy, to shield the professoriat, predictably was denounced by academic purists as betrayal. Presumably, Sproul regarded them as irresponsible.
3. Any academic who has served on a college committee on courses can testify that this function has been internalized, not abolished.
4. Title IX, for instance, has recently been interpreted in federal guidelines as forbidding universities from constructing new "cot" rooms in women's restrooms; since such facilities are not provided in university men's rooms, these benefactions are declared to violate the Civil Rights Act of 1964. (A few unconventional, forward-looking organizations such as the Hoover Institution in Palo Alto came to terms with this unusual provision by constructing "cot" rooms in male facilities. It now remains to be seen whether male scholars at Hoover can come up with "hot flashes.")

2. Richard W. Lyman: "Federal Regulation and Institutional Autonomy: A University President's View"

1. Stanford's current estimate is to spend some $950,000 to make its facilities accessible, of which a grant from the Department of Housing and Urban Development will cover $85,000. The remainder will come from the university's general funds.
2. For what follows, I am much indebted to an article based on a study of the Stanford University Medical Center done for the Alfred P. Sloan Foundation by Rosenzweig, Wilkes, and Freeman (1977).
3. At the state level, however, it has not been immune. For example, California law now requires that the Board of Medical Quality Assurance determine the length and content of curriculum offerings in human sexuality. Medical schools in California are now seeking repeal of this law.
4. Quotations are from the "Summary Statement . . . Sex Discrimination—Proposed HEW Regulation to Effectuate Title IX of the Education Amendments of 1972."

4. Robert L. Sproull: "Federal Regulation and the Natural Sciences"

1. One *must* have auditors; it is only a question of numbers. But the *creative* act of the scientist's imagination must not be diminished. After all, one definition of an auditor is "a person who comes onto the field of battle after the battle is over and shoots the wounded."

2. I admit that all of us in universities indulged in a considerable amount of ritual screaming in support of this persistence.

3. One senator has made considerable political hay by taking cheap shots at the *titles* of research projects, evidently unaware of how preoccupation with titles reveals his own superficiality. All scientists play the game of inventing titles that might get them "awards." My favorite is "Some Observations on the Anomalous Behavior of Photographic Plates in the Neighborhood of Crookes Tubes." What's that? The discovery of X-rays!

4. One of the chief difficulties in achieving sensible public and congressional attitudes to tolerable levels of carcinogens and appropriate methods of nuclear waste disposal is the circumstance that American schools produce no understanding of probability or of reasoning based on probability and statistics. Further, U.S. high schools do not even prepare the citizenry to deal with numbers of widely different orders of magnitude.

5. At the time of writing, the regulations have not yet been written, and they may not be written until after the effective date, 1 July 1979. Meanwhile, any individual who leaves the government after that date risks criminal penalties for non-compliance.

5. Miro M. Todorovich: "A Road to Stalemate—The Current State of Regulations"

1. A telling account of such practices can be found in an oral report to the Board of Higher Education (*Minutes of Proceedings*, 25 September 1972, p. 162) by Chancellor Robert J. Kirbee of the City University of New York:

"Mr. Pottinger of HEW's Office of Civil Rights exploded a small timebomb in the press at a meeting he held in New York to discuss a letter he had sent to me. It was an ultimatum [under the threat of cutoff of Federal funds] to the City University to provide certain data and to get assurance that we would allow access to the personnel files of City University for the purposes of HEW's Office of Civil Rights. This was followed by a long conference held in Washington by members of his staff, myself, the Deputy Chancellor, and Vice-Chancellor Meng. In August we came to a temporary resolution of the issues. The first issue which was resolved easily was that the City University would agree to provide the information, provided it was given anonymously. We would list individuals but not by name. The question of access to files was a stickier issue. That was finally resolved on the basis of the request of HEW that we allow them access to files of two departments of twenty-five members and that these files be made anonymous. A third thing that came out of it which was not a result of our negotiations was that HEW would not entertain individual complaints.

"These would go to the Equal Opportunity Commission, which has a different way of operating essentially through the courts. We are providing them with lists. What they will do from then on we don't know."

2. The commission moved under the authority given to it by Section 713 of the Civil Rights Act (CRA) of 1964 when it published, in December 1977, its proposed *Interpretation Regulation Guidelines for Remedial and/or Affirmative Action Appropriate under Title VII of the CRA* (29 CFR Part 1608).

3. "Item 1. An employer or other person subject to Title VII who has a reasonable basis for concluding that it might be held in violation of Title VII and who takes remedial and/or affirmative action reasonably calculated to avoid that result on the basis of such self-analysis *does not thereby violate Title VII with respect to any employee or applicant for employment who is denied an employment opportunity as a result of such action*. The lawfulness of such remedial and/or affirmative action program is not dependent upon an admission, or a finding, or evidence sufficient to prove that the employer or other person subject to Title VII taking such action has violated Title VII." [Italics added.]

4. "Item 2. The remedial and/or affirmative action programs contemplated by these Guidelines, whether taken by private employers or governmental employers or other persons covered by Title VII, *include the use of race, color, sex, and ethnic-conscious goals and timetables, ratios, or other numerical remedies intended to remedy the prior discrimination* against or exclusion of racial, sex or ethnic groups or to ensure that the employer's practices presently operate in a nondiscriminatory manner." [Italics added.]

5. To secure immunity for the suggested discriminatory action of employers, the proposed guidelines lean on the wording of Section 713 of Title VII, which provides, in part:

"No person should be subject to any liability or punishment for [or] on account of (1) the commission by such person of an unlawful employment practice if he pleads and proves that the act of omission complained of was in good faith, in conformity with, and in reliance on any written interpretation or opinion of the Commission."

6. A recent court action by Sears, Roebuck and Company shows that even this hope oversimplifies the problem. The giant retailer accuses the government of constantly changing the bottom line, thus making an acceptable voluntary compliance virtually impossible.

6. Nathan Glazer: "Regulating Business and Regulating the Universities: One Problem or Two?"

1. On Senators Goldwater and Tower, see Finn (1978:139), quoting "Minority Views of Senators Barry Goldwater and John G. Tower," National Defense Education Act Amendment of 1961 (S. Rept. 652, 87:1, p. 117): "If adopted, the legislation will mark the inception of aid, supervision and ultimately control of education in this country by Federal authorities."

Kingman Brewster, then president of Yale, has provided this controversy with one of its most eloquent images (Finn 1978:117): "Use of the leverage of the government dollar to accomplish objectives which have nothing to do with the purposes for which the dollar is given has become dangerously fashionable. . . . It might be called the 'now that I have bought the button, I have a right to design the coat' approach." For President Derek Bok of Harvard University, see Harvard University (1974–75).

2. Weaver (1978) has criticized this prevailing view, and I am inclined to accept his judgment. Much of the nurturant attitude of regulatory agencies, if not called for in its founding legislation, seems to have arisen mainly as a result of the decline of the industry they were regulating—e.g., railroads and shipbuilding.

3. And yet there are those who use the theory of the regulated capturing the regulators to argue that higher education doesn't have much to worry about. See Gellhorn and Boyer (1978:49):

"There are already some signs that higher education is following the patterns set by the regulated industries in their dealings with government agencies. The American Council on Education and the more specialized professional and academic associations are frequent, effective participants in the regulatory process. *The Chronicle of Higher Education* covers government regulatory stories as intensively as many industry trade journals do. And the capture of administrative agencies by the regulated industry seems to be well advanced in the field of higher education. Two university chancellors were appointed recently to the ranking positions dealing with higher education in the federal bureaucracy—Assistant Secretary for Education of the Department of HEW and U.S. Commissioner of Education."

An interesting position, which may reflect more the professional position of the two writers (lawyers)—who, whatever happens, will have plenty to do—rather than any reality. One notes that neither David Tatel, Director of the Office for Civil Rights of HEW, nor Eleanor Holmes Norton, Chairman of the Equal Employment Opportunity Commission, has any reason to be friendly towards higher education.

4. Important as the issue is—just how much discrimination in institutions of higher education was there, or is there, in the past and in the present, against women and minorities in admission, in employment, in promotion?—it cannot be settled here. But for some of the argument that the gross statistical standards used to demonstrate discrimination do not apply, see Glazer (1976), Equal Employment Advisory Council (1977), and Sowell (1978). For sophisticated efforts to test to what degree there was discrimination in higher education, see Freeman (1976), and Sowell (1976, 1975).

5. On this assessment of affirmative action, see van Alstyne and Coldren (1976:29). Where extra costs of administration imposed by government programs can be broken down in this study, equal employment opportunity costs are the highest. According to Spero (1978:2): "There seems to be almost universal agreement that federal laws and regulations dealing with non-discrimination in terms of both sex and minorities, equal employment opportunity and affirmative action have had more of an impact at campus level than other types of regulation."

6. We are all acquainted with this ploy, but for an account of how it works, see Searle (1978:211–12).

7. For an excellent account of the litigation and its implications for the autonomy of higher education, see Lloyd (1978).

8. See, on this point of how the best-laid plans to increase black enrollment at the University of Maryland are failing, "Intangibles Afflict University of Maryland's Recruitment of Blacks," *Washington Post* (18 February 1979).

9. Robert Bork (1978:175) writes: "In the discussion that followed this and the other talks [at the University Centers for Rational Alternatives conference], a prominent educator-administrator said government had to understand that university facul-

ties were selected on the principle of excellence and that this principle distinguished professors from garbage collectors, whose selection, one gathered, may properly be governed on grounds other than excellence. I was struck not only by the persistence of the claim to university uniqueness but by the apparent use of garbage collection as a metaphor for the activities of the rest of society."

7. Paul Seabury: "Epilogue—A Final Footnote"

1. Estelle Fishbein, General Counsel, Johns Hopkins University, to Dr. Charles McCarthy, National Institutes of Health, 5 February 1979. It should be pointed out that these particular new HEW regulations apparently are to be promulgated by the Secretary of Health, Education, and Welfare in a capricious manner, contrary to explicit congressional requirements—that is, without any statutorily required advance publication in the *Federal Register* to elicit public and professional comment. "I'll be judge, I'll be jury, said cunning old Fury."

2. Thus, as Soviet speechwriters are wont to say, "it is not accidental that" the HEW, when devising its model affirmative action plan for universities as a prototype for universal adoption, chose to negotiate it with the Berkeley campus of the University of California, and not, say, with Podunk State.

REFERENCES

Adams, Henry. 1948. *The Formative Years*, ed. Herbert Agar. London: Collins.

American Council on Education. 1963. *Twenty-six Campuses and the Federal Government*. Washington, DC: ACE.

Bailey, Cornelia W. 1978. "The Federal 504 Handicapped Access Regulations—A Case Study in Government–Higher Education Relations." Processed by Sloan Commission on Government and Higher Education (August). Washington, DC.

Bailey, Stephen. 1978. "The Peculiar Mixture: Public Norms and Private Space." In *Government Regulation of Higher Education*, ed. Walter C. Hobbs. Cambridge, MA: Ballinger.

Berelson, Bernard. 1960. *Graduate Education in the United States*. New York: McGraw-Hill.

Bonner, Thomas N. 1979. "V.A. vs. Wayne State's Weekend College." Letter-to-the-Editor, *New York Times* (16 February).

Bork, Robert H. 1978. "The Limits of Governmental Regulation." In *The University and the State*, ed. Sidney Hook, Paul Kurtz, and Miro Todorovich. Buffalo, NY: Prometheus Books.

Bowker, Albert H., and Morgan, Patrick M. 1977. "The Impact of Federal Regulations on the University of California, Berkeley." Unpublished (19 September).

Cartter, Allan. 1966. "Future Faculty Needs and Resources." In *The Improvement of College Teaching: Aids and Impediments*, ed. Charles Dobbins. Washington, DC: American Council on Education.

Conant, James Bryant. 1956. *The Citadel of Learning*. New Haven, CT: Yale University Press.

———. 1949. *Education in a Divided World*. Cambridge, MA: Harvard University Press.

Elliott, Ward. 1974. *The Rise of Guardian Democracy*. Boston: Harvard University Press.

Equal Employment Advisory Council. 1977. *Perspectives on Availability: A Symposium on Determining Protected Group Representation in Internal and External Labor Markets*. Washington, DC: EEAC.

Finn, Charles E., Jr. 1978. *Scholars, Dollars, and Bureaucrats*. Washington, DC: The Brookings Institution.

Fishbein, Estelle A. 1978. "The Academic Industry—A Dangerout Premise." In *Government Regulation of Higher Education*, ed. Walter C. Hobbs. Cambridge, MA: Ballinger.

Frankfurter, Felix. 1957. *Sweezy v. New Hampshire*, 354 US 234, 262 (1957) (Frankfurter, J., concurring).

Freeman, Richard B. 1976. *Black Elite*. New York: McGraw Hill.

Gellhorn, Ernest, and Boyer, Barry B. 1978. "The Academy as a Regulated Industry." In *Government Regulation of Higher Education*, ed. Walter C. Hobbs. Cambridge, MA: Ballinger.

Glazer, Nathan. 1976. *Affirmative Discrimination*. New York: Basic Books.

Gray, Bradford H.; Cooke, Robert A.; Tannenbaum, Arnold S. 1978. "Research Involving Human Subjects." *Science* 201 (20 September).

Harvard University. 1974–75. "The President's Report." Cambridge, MA: Harvard University Press.

Hobbs, Walter C., ed. 1978. *Government Regulation of Higher Education*. Cambridge, MA: Ballinger.

Hook, Sidney; Kurtz, Paul; Todorovich, Miro, eds. 1978. *The University and the State*. Buffalo, NY: Prometheus Books.

Lloyd, Crystal C. 1978. "*Adams v. Califano*: A Case Study in the Politics of Regulation." Processed by the Sloan Commission on Government and Higher Education (January). Washington, DC.

MacAvoy, Paul W., ed. 1978. *Unsettled Questions on Regulatory Reform*. Washington, DC: American Enterprise Institute.

Noll, Roger. 1978. Discussion in *Unsettled Questions on Regulatory Reform*, ed. Paul W. MacAvoy. Washington, DC: American Enterprise Institute.

Peter, Laurence J. 1979. *Peter's Quotations*. New York: Bantam Books.

Pierson, George Wilson, 1959. *Tocqueville in America*. Garden City, NY: Doubleday Anchor Books.

President's Science Advisory Committee. 1962. "The Gilliland Report" (12 December). In *Meeting Manpower Needs in Science and Technology*. Washington, DC: U.S. Superintendent of Documents.

Rosenzweig, Robert M.; Wilkes, Christopher; Freeman, Nancy. 1977. "Government: A Special Kind of Patron." *Stanford M.D.* 16, no. 3 (Fall).

Saunders, Charles B., Jr. 1976. "Easing the Burden of Federal Regulation: The Next Move Is Ours." *Educational Record* 57, no. 4.

Seabury, Paul. 1972. "HEW and the Universities." *Commentary* (February).

Searle, John R. 1978. "A More Balanced View." In *Government Regulation of Higher Education*, ed. Walter C. Hobbs. Cambridge, MA: Ballinger.

Sowell, Thomas. 1976. "Affirmative Action Reconsidered." *The Public Interest* 42 (Winter).

———. 1975. *Affirmative Action Reconsidered: Was It Necessary in Academia?* Washington, DC: American Enterprise Institute.

———. 1978. *American Ethnic Groups*. Washington, DC: The Urban Institute.

Spero, Irene K. 1978. *Government and Higher Education: A Summary of 21 Institutional Self-Studies*. Processed by the Sloan Commission on Government and Higher Education (January). Washington, DC.

Spriestersbach, D. C., and Farrell, William J. 1977. "Impact of Federal Regulations at a University." *Science* 198, no. 4312 (7 October).

Sumberg, Alfred D. 1978. "The Impact of Government Regulation on the Academic Occupation." In *Government Regulation of Higher Education*, ed. Walter C. Hobbs. Cambridge, MA: Ballinger.

van Alstyne, Carol. 1978. "The Costs to Colleges and Universities of Implementing Federally Mandated Social Programs." In *The University and the State*, ed. Sidney Hook, Paul Kurtz, and Miro Todorovich. Buffalo, NY: Prometheus Books.

———, and Coldren, Sharon L. 1976. *The Costs of Implementing Federally Mandated Social Programs at Colleges and Universities*. Washington, DC: American Council on Education.

Veysey, Laurence. 1965. *The Emergence of the American University*. Chicago: University of Chicago Press.

Weaver, Paul H. 1978. "Regulation, Social Policy, and Class Conflict." In *Regulating Business: The Search for an Optimum*. San Francisco: Institute for Contemporary Studies.

ABOUT THE AUTHORS

NATHAN GLAZER is Professor of Education and Sociology, Harvard University, and coeditor of *The Public Interest*. He was visiting scholar at the Russell Sage Foundation from 1977 to 1978. A former editor at Doubleday and Random House, he coauthored with Daniel P. Moynihan the book, *Beyond the Melting Pot* (1970). In *Parents, Teachers, and Children: Prospects for Choice in American Education* (1977), published by the Institute for Contemporary Studies, he wrote the chapter, "Public Education and American Pluralism." His recent books include *Affirmative Discrimination: Ethnic Inequality and Public Policy* (1976), and *The Urban Predicament* (1976), coedited with William Gorham.

ROBERT S. HATFIELD, Chairman and Chief Executive Officer of The Continental Group, Inc., personally supported that organization's economic education program entitled "The Role of Business in a Free Enterprise." In addition to his responsibilities as director of Johnson & Johnson, Inc., the New York Stock Exchange, and several major corporations, he serves as Trustee of the Committee for Economic Development, the Conference Board, and Cornell University, and is director of the Economic Development Council of New York City.

RICHARD W. LYMAN is President of Stanford University. A trustee of the Rockefeller Foundation and the Carnegie Foundation for the Advancement of Teaching, he is a member of the National Council for the Humanities, chairman of the Commission on the Humanities, and Honorary Fellow at the London School of Economics. A specialist in contemporary British history, he wrote *The First Labour Government, 1924* (reissued 1975), and coedited with Lewis W. Spitz, *Major Crises in Western Civilization* (1965).

PAUL SEABURY is a Visiting Scholar at the Hoover Institution, Stanford University, on leave from his position as Professor of Political Science at UC-Berkeley. He is National Vice Chairman of the University Centers for Rational Alternatives, a member of the Steering Committee, International Council on the Future of the University, and a member of the Council on Foreign Relations. He is editor of *Report on German Universities* (1978), and his writings include several books on international relations, "HEW and the Universities" (February 1972) and "The Idea of Merit" (December 1972), both published in *Commentary*. He also wrote the chapter, "Beyond Détente," in the Institute for Contemporary Studies book, *Defending America: Toward a New Role in the Post-Détente World* (1977).

ROBERT L. SPROULL, President and Chief Executive Officer of the University of Rochester, is a physicist with a long list of publications in solid state physics. Former chairman of the Consortium on Financing Higher Education, he is a trustee of the University of Rochester, a Fellow of the American Association for the Advancement of Science, and a member of the Sloan Commission on Government and Higher Education.

MIRO M. TODOROVICH, Assistant and Associate Professor of Physics at the Bronx Community College of the City University of New York, is chairman of the Academic Advisory Council of the National Legal Center for the Public Interest, Inc., in Washington, DC, and coordinator of the Committee on Academic Nondiscrimination and Integrity. He is cofounder and executive secretary of University Centers for Rational Alternatives and editor of UCRA's publication, *Measure*. The director of two NEH projects on contemporary education, and a widely published author in his fields of expertise, he is coeditor with Sidney Hook and Paul Kurtz of *The Idea of a Modern University* (1974), *The Ethics of Teaching and Research* (1977), and *University and the State—The Proper Role of Government in Higher Education* (1978).

CASPAR W. WEINBERGER, Vice President, Director, and General Counsel to the Bechtel Group of Companies and former Secretary of Health, Education, and Welfare, has also served as Director of the Office of Management and Budget and as Chairman of the Federal Trade Commission. A former chairman of the Republican State Central Committee of California, he was also chairman of the Assembly Committee on Government Organization, California State Legislature, and of the Commission on California State Government Organization and Economy, known as the Little Hoover Commission.

INDEX

PUBLICATIONS LIST

THE INSTITUTE FOR CONTEMPORARY STUDIES

260 California Street, San Francisco, California 94111

Catalog available upon request

BUREAUCRATS AND BRAINPOWER: GOVERNMENT REGULATION OF UNIVERSITIES

$6.95. 325 pages. Publication date: June 1979.
ISBN 0–917616–35–9
Library of Congress No. 79–51328

Contributors: Nathan Glazer, Robert S. Hatfield, Richard W. Lyman, Robert L. Sproull, Paul Seabury, Miro M. Todorovich, Caspar W. Weinberger

THE CALIFORNIA COASTAL PLAN: A CRITIQUE

$5.95. 199 pages. Publication date: March 1976.
ISBN 0–917616–04–9
Library of Congress No. 76–7715

Contributors: Eugene Bardach, Daniel K. Benjamin, Thomas E. Borcherding, Ross D. Eckert, H. Edward Frech III, M. Bruce Johnson, Ronald N. Lafferty, Walter J. Mead, Daniel Orr, Donald M. Pach, Michael R. Peevey.

THE CRISIS IN SOCIAL SECURITY: PROBLEMS AND PROSPECTS

$6.95. 220 pages. Publication date: April 1977; 2d ed., rev., 1978.
ISBN 0–917616–16–2/1977; 0–917616–25–1/1978
Library of Congress No. 77–72542

Contributors: Michael J. Boskin, George F. Break, Rita Ricardo Campbell, Edward Cowan, Martin S. Feldstein, Milton Friedman, Douglas R. Munro, Donald O. Parsons, Carl V. Patton, Joseph A.Pechman, Sherwin Rosen, W. Kip Viscusi, Richard J. Zeckhauser.

DEFENDING AMERICA: TOWARD A NEW ROLE IN THE POST-DETENTE WORLD

$13.95 (hardbound only). 255 pages. Publication date: April 1977 by Basic Books (New York).
ISBN 0–465–01585–9
Library of Congress No. 76–43479

Contributors: Robert Conquest, Theodore Draper, Gregory Grossman, Walter Z. Laqueur, Edward N. Luttwak, Charles Burton Marshall, Paul H. Nitze, Norman Polmar, Eugene V. Rostow, Leonard Schapiro, James R. Schlesinger, Paul Seabury, W. Scott Thompson, Albert Wohlstetter.

EMERGING COALITIONS IN AMERICAN POLITICS

$6.95. 530 pages. Publication date: June 1978.
ISBN 0–917616–22–7
Library of Congress No. 78–53414

Contributors: Jack Bass, David S. Broder, Jerome M. Clubb, Edward H. Crane III, Walter De Vries, Andrew M. Greeley, S. I. Hayakawa, Tom Hayden, Milton Himmelfarb, Richard Jensen, Paul Kleppner, Everett Carll Ladd, Jr., Seymour Martin Lipset, Robert A. Nisbet, Michael Novak, Gary R. Orren, Nelson W. Polsby, Joseph L. Rauh, Jr., Stanley Rothman, William A. Rusher, William Schneider, Jesse M. Unruh, Ben J. Wattenberg.

FEDERAL TAX REFORM: MYTHS AND REALITIES

$5.95. 270 pages. Publication date: September 1978.
ISBN 0–917616–32–4
Library of Congress No. 78–61661

Contributors: Robert J. Barro, Michael J. Boskin, George F. Break, Jerry R. Green, Laurence J. Kotlikoff, Mordecai Kurz, Peter Mieszkowski, John B. Shoven, Paul J. Taubman, John Whalley.

GOVERNMENT CREDIT ALLOCATION: WHERE DO WE GO FROM HERE?

$4.95. 208 pages. Publication date: November 1975.
ISBN O–917616–02–2
Library of Congress No. 75–32951

Contributors: George J. Benston, Karl Brunner, Dwight M. Jaffe, Omotunde E. G. Johnson, Edward J. Kane, Thomas Mayer, Allen H. Meltzer.

NEW DIRECTIONS IN PUBLIC HEALTH CARE: AN EVALUATION OF PROPOSALS FOR NATIONAL HEALTH INSURANCE

$6.95. 277 pages. Publication date: May 1976.
ISBN 0–917616–00–6
Library of Congress No. 76 - 40680

Contributors: Martin S. Feldstein, Thomas D. Hall, Leon R. Kass, Keith B. Leffler, Cotton M. Lindsay, Mark V. Pauly, Charles E. Phelps, Thomas C. Schelling, Arthur Seldon.

NO LAND IS AN ISLAND: INDIVIDUAL RIGHTS AND GOVERNMENT CONTROL OF LAND USE

$5.95. 221 pages. Publication date: November 1975.
ISBN 0–917616–03–0
Library of Congress No. 75–38415

Contributors: Benjamin F. Bobo, B. Bruce-Briggs, Connie Cheney, A. Lawrence Chickering, Robert B. Ekelund, Jr., W. Philip Gramm, Donald G. Hagman, Robert B. Hawkins, Jr., M. Bruce Johnson, Jan Krasnowiecki, John McClaughry, Donald M. Pach, Bernard H. Siegan, Ann Louise Strong, Morris K. Udall.

NO TIME TO CONFUSE: A CRITIQUE OF THE FORD FOUNDATION'S ENERGY POLICY PROJECT *A TIME TO CHOOSE AMERICA'S ENERGY FUTURE*

$4.95. 156 pages. Publication date: February 1975.
ISBN 0–917616–01–4
Library of Congress No. 75–10230

Contributors: Morris A. Adelman, Armen A. Alchian, James C. DeHaven, George W. Hilton, M. Bruce Johnson, Herman Kahn, Walter J. Mead, Arnold B. Moore, Thomas Gale Moore, William H. Riker.

ONCE IS ENOUGH: THE TAXATION OF CORPORATE EQUITY INCOME

$2.00. 32 pages. Publication date: May 1977.
ISBN 0–917616–23–5
Library of Congress No. 77–670132

Author: Charles E. McLure, Jr.

OPTIONS FOR U.S. ENERGY POLICY

$5.95. 317 pages. Publication date: September 1977.
ISBN 0–917616–20–0
Library of Congress No. 77–89094

Contributors: Albert Carnesale, Stanley M. Greenfield, Fred S. Hoffman, Edward J. Mitchell, William R. Moffat, Richard Nehring, Robert S. Pindyck, Norman C. Rasmussen, David J. Rose, Henry S. Rowen, James L. Sweeney, Arthur W. Wright.

PARENTS, TEACHERS, AND CHILDREN: PROSPECTS FOR CHOICE IN AMERICAN EDUCATION

$5.95. 336 pages. Publication date: June 1977.
ISBN 0–917616–18–9
Library of Congress No. 77–79164

Contributors: James S. Coleman, John E. Coons, William H. Cornog, Denis P. Doyle, E. Babette Edwards, Nathan Glazer, Andrew M. Greeley, R. Kent Greenawalt, Marvin Lazerson, William C. McCready, Michael Novak, John P. O'Dwyer, Robert Singleton, Thomas Sowell, Stephen D. Sugarman, Richard E. Wagner.

THE POLITICS OF PLANNING: A REVIEW AND CRITIQUE OF CENTRALIZED ECONOMIC PLANNING

$5.95. 367 pages. Publication date: March 1976.
ISBN 0–917616–05–7
Library of Congress No. 76–7714

Contributors: B. Bruce-Briggs, James Buchanan, A. Lawrence Chickering, Ralph Harris, Robert B. Hawkins, Jr., George W. Hilton, Richard Mancke, Richard Muth, Vincent Ostrom, Svetozar Pejovich, Myron Sharpe, John Sheahan, Herbert Stein, Gordon Tullock, Ernest van den Haag, Paul H. Weaver, Murray L. Weidenbaum, Hans Willgerodt, Peter P. Witonski.

PUBLIC EMPLOYEE UNIONS: A STUDY OF THE CRISIS IN PUBLIC SECTOR LABOR RELATIONS

$6.95. 251 pages. Publication date: June 1976; 2d ed., rev., 1977.
ISBN 0–917616–08–1/1976; ISBN 0–917616–24–3/1977
Library of Congress No. 76–17444

Contributors: A. Lawrence Chickering, Jack D. Douglas, Raymond D. Horton, Theodore W. Kheel, David Lewin, Seymour Martin Lipset, Harvey C. Mansfield, Jr., George Meany, Robert A. Nisbet, Daniel Orr, A. H. Raskin, Wes Uhlman, Harry H. Wellington, Charles B. Wheeler, Jr., Ralph K. Winter, Jr., Jerry Wurf.

REGULATING BUSINESS: THE SEARCH FOR AN OPTIMUM

$6.95. 260 pages. Publication date: April 1978.
ISBN 0–917616–27–8
Library of Congress No. 78–50678

Contributors: Chris Argyris, A. Lawrence Chickering, Penny Hollander Feldman, Richard H. Holton, Donald P. Jacobs, Alfred E. Kahn, Paul W. MacAvoy, Almarin Phillips, V. Kerry Smith, Paul H. Weaver, Richard J. Zeckhauser.

TARIFFS, QUOTAS, AND TRADE: THE POLITICS OF PROTECTIONISM

$6.95. 330 pages. Publication date: February 1979.
ISBN 0–917616–34–0
Library of Congress No. 78–66267

Contributors: Walter Adams, Ryan C. Amacher, Sven W. Arndt, Malcolm D. Bale, John T. Cuddington, Alan V. Deardorff, Joel B. Dirlam, Roger D. Hansen, H. Robert Heller, D. Gale Johnson, Robert O. Keohane, Michael W. Keran, Rachel McCulloch, Ronald I. McKinnon, Gordon W. Smith, Robert M. Stern, Richard James Sweeney, Robert D. Tollison, Thomas D. Willett.

THE THIRD WORLD: PREMISES OF U.S. POLICY

$5.95. 332 pages. Publication date: November 1978.
ISBN 0–917616–30–8
Library of Congress No. 78–67593

Contributors: Dennis Austin, Peter T. Bauer, Max Beloff, Richard E. Bissell, Daniel J. Elazar, S. E. Finer, Allan E. Goodman, Nathaniel H. Leff, Seymour Martin Lipset, Edward N. Luttwak, Daniel Pipes, Wilson E. Schmidt, Anthony Smith, W. Scott Thompson, Basil S. Yamey.

WATER BANKING: HOW TO STOP WASTING AGRICULTURAL WATER

$2.00. 56 pages. Publication date: January 1978.

ISBN 0-917616-26-X

Library of Congress No. 78-50766

Authors: Sotirios Angelides, Eugene Bardach.